Blackmail

Blackmail

Publicity and Secrecy in Everyday Life

Mike Hepworth
Department of Sociology,
University of Aberdeen

moxc

Routledge & Kegan Paul
London and Boston

First published in 1975
by Routledge & Kegan Paul Ltd
Broadway House, 68-74 Carter Lane,
London EC4V 5EL and
9 Park Street,
Boston, Mass. 02108, USA
Set in IBM Century by Pentagon Print,
Gresse Street, London, W1
and printed in Great Britain by
Lowe & Brydone (Printers) Ltd
Thetford, Norfolk
ISBN 0 7100 8235 5(C)
      0 7100 8236 3(P)

For Marian

Contents

Acknowledgments

Early traces of this book may be found in Deviants in disguise: blackmail and social acceptance, a paper I wrote for the third National Deviancy Symposium at the University of York, in 1969, and later published in 'Images of Deviance', edited by Stanley Cohen, Penguin Books, 1971. In addition, part of the historical argument in Chapter 1 has appeared in The British conception of blackmail, 'International Journal of Criminology and Penology', vol. 3, no. 1, 1975.

I should like to thank everyone who took time out to discuss the problem of blackmail, and the many others who wrote helpful letters. I am especially grateful for the encouragement of my friends and colleagues.

M.H.

Introduction

The criminal offence of blackmail is universally feared. By many in this country it is 'considered the foulest of crimes — far crueller than most murders because of its cold-blooded premeditation and repeated torture of the victim; incomparably more offensive to the public conscience than the vast majority of other offences which the law seeks to punish'.[1]

What I have tried to do in the pages ahead is to track down the main sources of this offence 'to the public conscience': to spell out more clearly the nature of the fear of blackmail, and to draw attention to the quality of evidence available to support the conclusion that blackmail is a serious threat to social order, 'a crime which must be stamped out'.

At the present time the criminal law recognises three main kinds of punishable offence: blackmail by way of crude physical intimidation, blackmail involving threats not to accuse someone of a criminal offence, and reputational blackmail where the offender threatens to reveal potentially discrediting information concerning the victim to a wider audience. In all instances blackmail is defined as the unlawful manipulation of an advantageous situation to pressurise victims into parting unwillingly with cash, goods, or services. When, therefore, blackmail is publicly stigmatised as a social evil it is possible for commentators to be referring to one, or even a combination of three different methods of terrorisation. Although these offences are interrelated, as we shall see in Chapter 1, we shall be mainly concerned in this book with the third type of public menace — to which the above questions actually refer — blackmail commanding a ransom on the

1

reputation of the victim.[2]

Not surprisingly, unbiased information detailing the 'real' nature and extent of reputational blackmail is hard to find, yet we need look no further than the world of popular crime fiction for dramatic representations of the personal and social havoc it can create. Anders Bodelsen, for example, offers a compelling portrayal of the vulnerability of the victim in modern society when he describes blackmail within the higher reaches of a motor manufacturing firm in Denmark.[3]

Towards the end of a drinking session Mork, an up and coming manager working on an advanced car project, accompanies some students he has just met to a party, where he rapidly becomes ill-at-ease in the unfamiliar surroundings. He has a few more drinks and then leaves the uncongenial gathering in a car secretly 'borrowed' from a fellow guest. Driving home through the heavy snow he accidentally knocks down an elderly bicyclist and leaving the casualty dead hurries on to a world of unremitting personal tension. Mork's life is now totally overshadowed by the fear that discovery will inevitably bring social ruin; at every turn he expects to encounter Hostrup, the owner of the car, who he believes will denounce him as the mysterious hit-and-run driver featured in the news. When Hostrup finally emerges out of obscurity, he blackmails Mork into getting him a job in his organisation : a part-share in Mork's successful career.

Bodelsen shows that it is Mork's complete absorption in his career which makes him, for a time at least, such an easy target for the blackmailer. Immediately after the accident he decides his life, like the life of the old man, has come to end. Although Mork feels guilty, his main task is not to invent excuses for his actions but to 'defend himself'. He must work behind the scenes to sustain an untarnished public image so that, when Hostrup eventually makes his fateful appearance, Mork is ready to pay the price of his silence in order to secure the future.

In contrast, Alan Hardy, the English narrator in a second blackmail novel, is not so fortunate.[4] The story opens with his career as a top television personality in ruins. He has been photographed in bed with a girl of fourteen and the evidence is posted off to his wife and employers, none of whom prove sympathetic. Sustained by the reflection that anyone who is rich and in the public eye must live with the expectation of blackmail, Hardy seeks out other, yet undiscovered, victims who furnish him with sufficient evidence to locate and confront the mass blackmailer. Unabashed, the culprit presents himself in the guise of a moral crusader — a man ultimately on the side of the angels, holding out a mirror to his reputable clients so they can catch a glimpse of their true unworthy selves.

Adopting this kind of moral imagery, the author is able to capture two highly ambiguous attributes of the master blackmailer. First, whilst the blackmailer is stigmatised because he sets a price upon his willingness to keep a discreditable secret,[5] he also attracts massive disapproval because he is prepared to betray secrets in the 'public interest'. Second, in spite of the negative reaction to betrayal, a major source of interest in blackmail stems from the publicity value of what are often categorised as 'grubby' aspects of the victim's private life. Fundamentally the offender becomes a trader in what Alan Hardy calls 'virulent' information; grubby secrets are transformed into 'virulent' information partly through the efforts of the blackmailer who assesses their potential for arousing the public censure of his outwardly respectable clients.

This tortuous cultural theme underwrites a thriller by Victor Canning: 'The Scorpio Letters'.[6] However, unlike Mork and Alan Hardy, the hero of Canning's tale is not himself blackmailed; he discovers accidentally that a respected relative has been paying blackmail for years to cover up a trivial sexual indiscretion. Filled with bitterness against whoever is responsible for those years of torment, he traces the letters back to the master blackmailer, Scorpio, whom he finds making a luxurious living out of an extensive international clientele.

As in the case of the Alan Hardy story, the moot point of moral surveillance is not ignored. Although the blackmailer is presented as an evil profiteering criminal — the focal point of a communications network transmitting discreditable information — he is nevertheless allowed to make some claim to moral status. Scorpio has rejected his early years of poverty and memories of the condescension of the socially advantaged whose private lives he knows are sometimes suspect: he feels justified in advancing his own interest at the expense of the failings of those he feels can afford to pay on his terms. He sends his son to a public school and is shown writing the boy a letter urging him to work ceaselessly at his powers of observation in order to formulate accurate and profitable judgments of those around him. By the same token, Scorpio grinds down the lives of his victims and to deal with the ultimate menace the hero must put aside his basic sense of decent fair play, continually reminding himself of the unhappiness inflicted on others. In the end, because the hero must uphold the 'status quo', Scorpio can only be treated as an utterly repellent figure who has placed himself well beyond the boundaries of common human decency.

All three crime novels show blackmail to be an exploitative activity reaching out into the very heart of the legitimate rat-race for wealth and status, positing a threat to conventional relations between social classes. At the same time Victor Canning's blackmailer is only marginally conscious of the humiliation of his poverty-stricken past whilst Ted Lewis's fictional character Plender is literally obsessed with the need to square his version of the social account.[7]

Under cover of a private detection agency Plender runs a highly rationalised blackmailing organisation on behalf of the 'Movement', an obscure fascistic conspiracy. Plender sees himself as a self-made man and is preoccupied with the pursuit of success: his ability, through blackmail, to exercise a sense of power over victims from a higher social class. This wider concern with self-aggrandisement is channelled into the pursuit of a personal vendetta against Knott whom Plender has hated since grammar-school days. Knott is now a successful photographer and Plender gains ascendancy over him through knowledge of his intense personal involvement in sexual perversions. Motivated by memories of boyish insults and other injuries at the hands of the socially superior Knott family, Plender threatens to make the secret public, thus destroying Knott's marriage and progressively reducing him to a conscience-stricken shadow of his former self. Ted Lewis interprets the present relationship of the two men in terms of the relations of the past; blackmail assumes the form of a mini class war with disastrous consequences for both parties.

So much for fictional accounts of blackmail — at least for the time being. Inevitably they suggest a series of important questions: how valid are these descriptions of this dangerous activity? ; in what ways do actual prosecutions reaching the criminal courts resemble these creations? ; what kinds of social consideration prompt certain individuals to accede to the demands of the blackmailer? ; and under what conditions do potential blackmailers conclude that it is appropriate or justifiable to threaten to reveal someone's private secrets to a wider audience for cash or some other consideration? It is to these substantive issues, revolving around conceptions of publicity and secrecy in everyday life, that we shall turn in our exploration of the continuing sense of unease reputational blackmail has provoked in Britain throughout the last hundred years.

At the time of writing newspapers record the blackmailing of an unnamed middle-aged man for sexual offences he had not committed. The court appearance of a fifteen-year-old girl revealed the victim's endurance of almost two years of torment and anxiety; a cumulative sum of £1,720 had been paid out to ensure that she would not broadcast to the world the fiction that sexual relations had taken place between them. According to reports the victim had been particularly anxious to protect his invalid mother from the strain of the scandalous publicity. Although only a small proportion of the blackmail money was recovered, one important outcome, from the victim's point of view, was the vindication of his reputation. He had genuinely believed the teenage blackmailer would carry out her threats; innocent of any physical act of deviation his anxiety clearly played around the adverse interpretation he felt fellow community members would be likely to place upon threatened public statements by the actual offender. In effect he was being made to purchase back the reputation appropriated by the blackmailer as an income-producing asset.[8]

For *the victim*, whether in fiction or in life, blackmail is a sensitive business. Summing up at the close of the celebrated 'Mr A Case' on 28 November 1924, Lord Darling observed,[9]

> it is ordinarily called blackmailing, to demand money of a person with menaces so that he parts with it against his will, not really consenting but because he has got into such a tight place that he feels he can do nothing else; that is what the law calls stealing, and this is why blackmailers are punished as they are.

We have already noted that it is because apparently respectable people occasionally find themselves in 'a tight place' reflecting adversely on their reputations that blackmail, one touchstone of public moral sensibility, assumes its peculiar ambiguity. For these very reasons victims are naturally reluctant to disclose their involvement and short of actual participation in an offence it is almost impossible for the researcher to discover detailed first-hand accounts of the experience of blackmail. A situation compounded by the reluctance of public officials and other interested parties, aware of the location of concealed information about blackmail transactions, to provide access to this confidential material, or even to involve themselves in any kind of discussion; the very social factors which make successful blackmail possible, impose significant restrictions upon the research task.

These overall social constraints necessarily affect the quality and quantity of *published* material available. There are no non-fictional works devoted entirely to the subject in Britain. Most of the numerous academic analyses of crime and deviance, both in Britain and the USA, contain nothing more than passing references to blackmail; and where extended accounts exist, they consist for the most part of a handful of popularised case-histories which perhaps add to our appreciation of human perversity without enhancing our understanding of blackmail itself. For instance, in one of the few explicit publications, Basil Tozer's journalistic 'Confidence Crooks and Blackmailers' of 1929,[10] only 29 out of 236 pages contain any descriptive material; and although J.C. Ellis's 'Blackmailers & Co', published slightly earlier,[11] offers probably the most extensive coverage for the period, it is hardly exhaustive. The existing literature, therefore, is fragmentary, treating blackmail either as an undetected widespread menace to western civilisation or lumping it exclusively together with descriptions of the so-called 'blackmailable' sexual deviations.[12]

Introduction

In focussing attention directly on the blackmail transaction itself, I have brought to light a wide selection of prosecutions reported in the British press over the last hundred years. In terms of the major questions outlined above, I have attempted to relate this and other accessible data to our commonsense understandings of the role of blackmail in modern society. Since blackmail is peculiarly sensitive, precise references to the sources of cases occurring after 1939 have been omitted, and with regard to the whole period under review, very few participants have been identified. Nevertheless, except where stated, none of the actors in the events to be recounted are fictional, and all the events are 'true' in that certain people suffered and lived out the consequences.

Chapter 1

The Concept
of Blackmail

Blackmail is possible only when individuals are discreditable.

Laud Humphries[1]

Activities we now punish as reputational blackmail have been recorded throughout history, though it was not until relatively recently that the law set the seal of 'criminalisation'[2] on the offence. The Newgate Calendar for 1779 describes the conviction and execution of James Donally for extorting money 'by the vilest of all insinuations, from the Honourable Charles Fielding, second son of the Earl of Denbigh'. Donally had attempted to defend himself against an accusation of blackmail on the grounds that Fielding had tried to 'commit a most foul crime' (a homosexual act). True to the legal tradition of their age, however, the judges at Donally's subsequent trial did not define his offence as blackmail (in the sense we now use the term): they considered that extortion, using a threatened accusation, could only be classified as one form of highway robbery.[3]

Prior to the nineteenth century, the word 'blackmail' was commonly reserved to denote extortion (theft and robbery) involving physical intimidation.[4] Medieval society, for example, had its run of outlaws skilled in the practice of extortion. John Bellamy has recently shown from his examination of early court records, how criminals frequently banded together for utilitarian purposes, extortion being a particularly favoured means of profiting from the disorder of the times.[5] He records that 'Robert Fraunceys of Hardstoff (Nottinghamshire) who was visited on 26 December 1331 by an envoy of Robert le Sauvage called William del Hethe and was asked for forty shillings felt so threatened that he left his house and did not return for a long time'. Outlaws became so well known in some localities there was no need for face-to-face confrontation with the victim, a 'threatening letter by the hand of a

7

messenger would suffice'. Moreover the practice of extortion was by no means the prerogative of outlaws. Bellamy also shows that officials nominally responsible for law and order were often well-known extortionists. One significant medieval official, the hundred bailiff, 'acquired a reputation for extortion by threatening to arrest people arbitrarily, impounding beasts wrongfully, and letting men off army and jury service'. Justices of oyer and terminer, and of the peace, were equally not always noted for an overriding sense of principle, and it was widely accepted that the numerous applicants for posts of prison keeper were attracted by opportunities to extort.[6]

From the Middle Ages through to the last century, extortion by criminals and non-criminals alike was typically described as the payment of 'black mail' ('black money') enforced through threats to life, limb or property. However, during the latter half of the century, an emerging awareness of the need to safeguard individual reputation against threats by a potential blackmailer began to make itself felt; an awareness reflected in a change in the public image of the blackmailer away from the physically menacing outlaw, bandit,[7] highway robber, or even corrupt official, towards the subtler yet equally menacing trader on quite a different order of human weakness. By 1968 it was possible for Edward Griew to write in his 'Introduction' to the blackmail section of the new Theft Act that the word itself was commonly understood by 'laymen' to mean 'the obtaining of some advantage by the use of improper threats, especially threats to make use of information discreditable to the victim'. Griew also observed that although the layman's use of the word 'blackmail' was 'looser than the lawyer's', laymen and lawyer did not greatly differ in their definition and understanding of what amounted to blackmail.[8]

Indeed, we now appear to have reached a stage in our social arrangements where imputations of blackmail can be triggered off by a series of apparently widely divergent social situations. In the press the word has been frequently used to indicate what almost amounts to a new typology of blackmailing in modern life: from time to time we must all have read reports of,

'Official' blackmail
'Political' blackmail
'Economic' blackmail
'Liberty' blackmail
'Moral' blackmail
'Juvenile' blackmail
'Sexual' blackmail
'Literary' blackmail
'Emotional' blackmail,

and a host of others, less easily abbreviated, but no less telling in their implicit condemnation. Not all these variations on a theme are, of course, defined as criminal offences, but they can (and sometimes do), incorporate or conceal blackmail against reputation.

One reason for the allegedly concealed nature of modern blackmail is increased opportunity for potential blackmailers to select from an expanding and often subtler range of threats; the growth of commercial-industrial society has had the side-effect of extending the blackmailer's repertoire.

On one level there is no mistaking the following threat, albeit fanciful, contained in this letter received by the Prince of Wales in December 1885:

> Your Royal Highness — Take these letters aside
> and read in private, as they contain certain
> matters concerning an attempt on your life.
> For certain reasons which you will know in
> good time, I leave out the preliminaries.
> Five men were required to carry out the
> order for your assassination, and for that
> person lots were drawn by 27 men. The first
> men, of whom I am one, were sworn, and after
> being bound to secrecy by the most fearful
> oaths, and being well supplied with money
> from the society's funds, we sailed for
> England, and arrived in London a few days
> ago.

Money was demanded to halt these sinister arrangements.

The two letters received by the Prince were passed on to the police who made an appointment to pay £750 to a woman. Observation of the rendezvous ultimately led to the arrest of the conspirators: an unemployed photographer and his wife. Both were then charged with attempting to extort money with menaces.[9]

A prosecution following the wake of certain events in Widnes in 1898 affords a useful point of comparison, illustrating the more recent problems encountered by the legal profession when attempting to define a specific act as blackmail against reputation. During the course of the incident which led to a court appearance, the alleged blackmailer had given the complainant a signed note:

> Received on account from . . . and given on condition I don't
> report [signed by the defendant].

It was stated in court that the prosecutor and another man had gone into a field to check on some sheep. A third person appeared and pointed to a fast moving object which the prosecutor promptly shot dead; it was later discovered he had killed a cock pheasant. By chance, a fourth man was driving past the field in a trap when he heard the shot. Pulling up he saw what had been hit and, as a good neighbour, advised the marksman he would have to report him for not having a gun licence. A long argument ensued.

The owner of the gun apologised to his accuser for an impulsive act, adding the rider that he did not want their argument to get into the papers as people would think he was a poacher. Thus persuaded, the would-be blackmailer agreed not to pursue the matter provided he was given £3. Later, he apparently agreed to accept the lesser sum of a sovereign, together with the gun, and it was at this point in the transaction that he signed the receipt which eventually passed into the hands of the police as evidence for the prosecution.

Following an extensive debate over the propriety of the charge under Elizabethan and Victorian law, the judge stopped the case. Finding the defendant not guilty and dismissing the charge, he stated, 'We think it was a business transaction'.[10]

Incidents such as those at Widnes provide some insight into the everyday contexts from which statements, occurrences, and cues are extracted by external agents of the law in order to create the drama of a public prosecution. A complex situation of this kind confronts the police with the task of amassing appropriate evidence to prove a criminal threat has been made. As we have seen, they are not always successful.

On the other hand, Victorian judges did not always find it difficult to distinguish an unambiguous threat of blackmail from a legitimate commercial proposition. Five years before the judge dismissed the case in Widnes, a one-time gardener on the estates of Viscount Clifden was sentenced to five years penal servitude for sending a letter containing the following threats against his former employer:

> I now beg to inform your lordship that unless this notice is withdrawn [he had been dismissed because of dissatisfaction with his services] I shall apply for £1,000 damages and disclose the whole thing, or I shall take £500, and leave the place and say nothing.

The charge came under the statute providing that anyone sending letters containing accusations of this kind (typically unspecified in this report of the case in 'The Times'), with intent to extort money, was liable to penal servitude for life. In passing a lighter sentence Mr Justice Hawkins unburdened himself as follows:

The crime of writing such a letter was a very grave one, and many a man before had been sent into penal servitude for a much longer term than he proposed to send the prisoner. No statement had been made on the part of the prosecution to aggravate or mitigate the sentence which ought to be pronounced. He therefore must act upon the opinion which he had formed on the depositions before him. *In justice to the safety of the community, he could not allow the prisoner's offence to go without serious punishment.* If he were to pass a more nominal sentence, in order that the prisoner's friends might send him to America, it would be holding out an encouragement to people, instead of a warning to people that an offence of this kind could not be committed without serious consequences. (My emphasis).

Whilst the more obvious physical threats may be made with varying degrees of credibility, it is usually not too difficult for officials to decide whether an *illegal threat* has actually been made. With regard to reputational blackmail, the problem of interpreting the evidence and the law, as we shall see, looms much larger. Nevertheless, acknowledgment of these difficulties did not prevent nineteenth-century lawyers and judges from unequivocally defining blackmail as a threat to public order. In 1853 a barrister-at-law briefly drew public attention to what he believed to be a general decline in physical molestation and an attendant increase in threats against reputation.

So near to our own time did the payment of blackmail approach in Scotland [he wrote] that an instance of it was related to me by a person who had been present. Mr Cameron, the late Provost of Banff, told me that he distinctly remembered when a boy going with his father's grieve [bailiff] to pay black-mail to a highland Chief. Part of it he recollected was given in oatmeal. But, indeed, when it is considered that a hundred years have scarcely elapsed since nearly the whole of the Highlands were under feudal authority almost independent of government, and since a Civil War was waging that shook the country to its foundations, it cannot be surprising that an elderly man should remember the time when a quiet country gentleman was glad to compound for safety by paying a tax to robbers.

Change, argues the writer, is in the air. The amount of violence, including extortion, is declining as life becomes physically safer; but new dangers threaten an urban society.[12]

The Concept of Blackmail

The law of blackmail

As I have suggested, blackmail was only gradually absorbed into statute. The first enactment to incorporate an explicit reference to blackmail — the Elizabethan Act of 1601 — clearly defined the offence as a form of robbery:[13]

> Many of her Majesty's subjects, dwelling . . . within the counties of Cumberland, Northumberland, Westmoreland, and the Bishoprick of Duresme have been taken, some forth of their own Houses, and some in travelling by the Highway, or otherwise, and carried . . . as Prisoners, and kept barbarously and cruelly until they have been redeemed by great Ransome: and . . . there have been many Incursions, Roads Robberies, and burning and spoiling of Towns, Villages and Houses within the said Counties, so that divers . . . of her Majesty's Subjects, in the said Counties . . . have been enforced to pay a certain Rate of Money, corn, cattle or other consideration, commonly called . . . Black-mail, . . . to the End thereby to be . . . freed, protected and kept in Safety from the Danger of such as do usually rob and steal in those Parts.

News of limited disturbances of public order in the border counties prompted Elizabethan response and 'Black-mail' first received statutory recognition as a popular term for describing localised disorder. Not until the eighteenth century did the law of blackmail begin to take on a wider significance, in 1722 the notorious Waltham Black Act,[14] also a product of heightened awareness of localised social disturbance, paved the way for a new interpretation of robbery and larceny:[15]

> several ill-designing and disorderly persons have of late associated themselves under the name of 'Blacks' . . . and have likewise solicited several of His Majesty's subjects, with promises of money, or other rewards, to join with them, and have sent letters in fictitious names, to several persons, demanding venison and money, and threatening some great violence, if such, their unlawful demands, should be refused, or if they should be interrupted in, or prosecuted for such, their wicked practices, and have actually done great damage to several persons, who have either refused to comply with such demands, or have endeavoured to bring them to justice, to the great terror of His Majesty's peaceable subjects.

We have seen that extortion by means of threatening letters was not new to the eighteenth century — reports of the offence recur throughout the Middle Ages and later — but during this period it was seen to be an increasingly common danger and 'it was probably partly for this reason that the courts put a liberal construction on the relevant section of the Black Act'.[16] Throughout the reigns of George I and George II, various statutes came into being punishing this method of extortion with seven years' transportation. If the victim could be shown to have been threatened with murder, the punishment was death.[17] The Waltham Black Act thus made way for the addition of a second interpretative strand to the traditional legal equation of blackmail with robbery and theft: blackmail involving verbal and written threats to *accuse* someone of an offence, regardless of whether he had actually committed any crime. Although blackmail, robbery and theft remained interrelated, their 'criminological significance' was beginning to change.

When blackmail cases came to their attention, members of the judiciary gradually became interested in the degree of criminality evident in threats to accuse. What, they wondered, were the inherent qualities of these threats? Under what conditions were they likely to induce in the victim a state of terror? How could this state of terror best be measured? A short answer to all these questions was that the state of fear had to be sufficiently strong to overcome the victim's will, thus causing him to part reluctantly with some of his possessions.

A revised definition of the vulnerable victim was necessary to complement this slowly changing concept of the blackmailer's power. Debate over the general problem arose within the context of differing prosecutions under three disparate areas of common law: constructive robbery, extortion, and larceny by intimidation.[18] Our discussion does not require an elaboration of these frequently technical arguments except to underscore the fact that the three concepts were riddled with ambiguities, transforming the interpretation of the law into a hazardous enterprise. For us the kernel of the matter was precisely identified by Justice Ashurst in 1796: 'Terror is of two kinds; namely, a terror which leads the minds of the party to apprehend an injury to his person, or a terror which leads him to apprehend an injury to his character'.[19]

Of course, the argument that the anticipation of injury to character constituted an adequate threat in law to warrant punishment, hardly resolved the issue. The wider problem lay in determining the nature of individual character and its relation to the social order. In terms of the varieties of terror considered most likely to 'overcome a firm and constant mind' it was decided that reputation was the strategic factor. Recognition that threats did not have to be backed by fear of personal violence to unsettle a man was accompanied by the acknowledgment that individual reputations required protection. The search for some kind of measure of the degree of force a reputational blackmailer could effectively employ against his victim initially rested with the illegal employment of threats to accuse the victim of a punishable criminal offence. Other kinds of threats could surely be handled privately by the recipient out of court. They were not regarded as sufficiently serious to warrant the intervention of the state. W.H.D. Winder notes in his definitive paper on the historical development of the law of blackmail that towards the end of the eighteenth century 'the definition of robbery was relaxed to make it include the obtaining of a chattel as an immediate consequence of a present threat to accuse of unnatural crime'. The case of 'R.v. Jones' in 1776 established that a threatened accusation of sodomy constituted robbery because the judges also detected the presence of the important additional element of *physical force*. [20] However, eight years later Justice Ashurst gave the opinion in 'R.v. Hickman' that 'a threat to accuse a man of having committed the greatest of all crimes' was 'sufficient force to constitute the crime of robbery by putting in fear'. 'To most men', he added, 'the idea of losing their fame and reputation is equally, if not more terrific than the dread of personal injury'. [21]

Once the precedent had been established that the state had a legitimate interest in the fact that men could be put in fear for their reputations by threatened accusations of serious criminal offences, whether physical force was present or not, it was but a short step to extending the definition of blackmail to include *any* kind of threatened accusation. Historically the crucial formal milestone was a separate, though not unrelated piece of legislation, the Libel Act of 1843.

For the first time 'blackmail in its less gross forms', as Winder puts it, was made a criminal offence. This did not mean the thorny problem of providing an unambiguous definition of 'menaces' had been resolved. What it did mean was that under the Libel Act the characteristic feature of blackmail now familiar to us all — threatened exposure of the victim — was formally recognised as a social hazard. Baron Parke provided the classic definition of libel in 1840: since that time the essence of libel has remained the publication of information 'calculated to injure the reputation of another by exposing him to hatred, contempt or ridicule'. [22] The 1843 Act offered protection to *individual reputation* against those publishing 'or threatening to publish, or proposing to abstain or prevent from publishing, a libel in order to extort money or some other valuable thing'. The offence was defined as a misdemeanour 'punishable by imprisonment not exceeding three years'. [23] Thus a third interpretive strand, albeit from an external source, was added to the statutory law of blackmail. By the mid-nineteenth century, reputation had come to be viewed as potentially vulnerable to any manner of public statement, always providing evidence could be obtained proving such statements were likely to expose their subjects to 'hatred, ridicule or contempt'. [24]

'Hard' evidence concerning the number and nature of actual blackmail cases influencing legal opinion at this time is difficult, if not impossible, to obtain.[25] Certainly, few of the contemporary or more recent studies of Victorian criminality contain detailed references to the offence, neither are the criminal statistics much help. Nevertheless, it is clear that by the turn of the century, criminal blackmail comprised the three different forms of behaviour listed earlier:

1 blackmail through physical threats.
2 blackmail through threats to accuse someone of a criminal offence.
3 blackmail by means of threats to broadcast any discreditable statement.

In November 1885, Mr Justice Wills gave his opinion that 'he and all Her Majesty's Judges looked upon offences of this nature as the most serious known to the law'. Persons with weak temperaments 'had been known to commit suicide in consequence of unfounded charges . . . being made against them'.[26] A situation had emerged where some commentators were prepared to classify blackmail as a 'private crime': one of a group of offences comprising 'acts and omissions that are injurious to society as a whole, not by attacking the primary or secondary functions of the State, but by injuring its individual members, and so imparing its fabric by a process of attrition'.[27]

Good reputation, an increasingly significant mainstay of conventional order, was in effect defined as a vulnerable entity; a source both of social weakness and of strength, meriting the protection of the criminal courts. Whatever the areas of disagreement and doubt, the concept of 'menaces' had been progressively enlarged to include a much wider range of threats than eighteenth century lawyers would have conceived as either possible or desirable. Everyday private matters of personal reputation had been translated into matters affecting the public interest.

The motley accumulation of eighteenth- and nineteenth-century law on blackmail culminated in three consolidating sections of the Larceny Act, 1916; 'an ill assorted collection of legislative bric-a-brac put together with scissors and paste'.[28] A new code of blackmail was not established; instead each section attempted to draw together historical themes underpinning the gradual emergence of these varying forms, for this reason Sections 29, 30, and 31[29] have always been considered unsatisfactory by legal critics. Three qualitatively distinct kinds of behaviour were collectively and without precision, defined as 'demanding money with menaces'. Whilst there was considerable agreement that the threat of reputational blackmail constituted a new menace to the body politic, there was correspondingly less agreement on the way of defining the danger in law.

Pointing a way through the thicket of legal anomalies and blurred categories of offence, Glanville Williams argued that the 'principle of division' between Sections 29, 30 and 31 was 'that of punishment'.[30] An offender convicted of a felony under Section 29 was 'liable to penal servitude for life', regardless of whether the threats used were of 'violence, injury or accusation'. Under Section 30, the felonious concept of 'menaces' or 'force' was also extended to include less tangible threats *provided the intent was to steal*, though here the maximum penalty was five years' penal servitude; whereas with regard to Section 31, where the source of offence was defined as threats to *expose the victim* (incorporating the relevent area of the Libel Act, 1843), blackmail was defined less seriously as a misdemeanour carrying a maximum penalty of only two years' imprisonment. The most significant result of this confusion was that those suspected of apparently similar criminal actions could be prosecuted and punished with reference to different sections of the statute prescribing, as we have seen, qualitatively distinct forms of blackmail. If the police, lawyers, and members of the judiciary seemed sometimes unsure of the precise illegal status of some of the alleged offences coming to light throughout the period covered by the Act of 1916, we should not be surprised to find members of the lay public expressing a similar sense of confusion when called upon to justify certain of their actions before a criminal court.

When, in 1966, the Criminal Law Revision Committee reported on the law of theft, it stressed that legally the offence of blackmail did not exist. Blackmail was a term commonly applied to 'the group of offences of demanding money with menaces and similar conduct'. Over the years, it was felt, a series of reinterpretations of the concept of 'menaces' had resulted in the creation of the relative new offence of blackmail:[31]

> It was originally regarded as not a particularly serious offence, as is shown by the fact that the maximum penalty is only two years' imprisonment. But now the courts have given a greatly extended meaning to 'menaces' in S 29 (1) (i), so that it covers almost any kind of threat. Lord Wright defined it as meaning 'threats of action detrimental to or unpleasant to the person addressed'. ('Thorne Motor Trade Association' (1937) A.C. 797, 817, 26 (R.App. R.51,67).) This extension has had the result that ordinary blackmail, provided that the threat is contained in a letter, is punishable with imprisonment for life. This is in general acceptable to public opinion owing to the far greater odium in which the offence is now commonly held.

Members of the Committee decided that a return to 'first principles' was in order 'to consider as a matter of policy what kinds of conduct would amount to blackmail'. Because blackmail was essentially an 'offence of dishonesty' the following definition was proposed to replace the categories of 1916:

> A person is guilty of blackmail if, with a view to gain for himself or another or with intent to cause loss to another, he makes any *unwarranted* demand with menaces; and for this purpose a demand with menaces is unwarranted unless the person making it does so in the belief —
> (a) that he has *reasonable* grounds for making the demand; and
> (b) that the use of the menaces is a proper means of reinforcing the demand.

It was recommended the term 'menaces' should be retained in new legislation because it carried stronger connotations of socially unacceptable behaviour than the word 'threats'. 'Menaces' should include demands made as the price of not revealing knowledge of discreditable conduct by the victim. The Committee assumed the 'true blackmailer *will know* that he had no reasonable grounds for demanding money as the price of keeping his victim's secret: the person with a genuine claim will be guilty unless *he believes* that it is proper to use the menaces to enforce his claim'. (My emphases).[32] The lesson of the past was that attempts to formulate an *objective* test of blackmail posed almost insuperable difficulties; the important *subjective* test of the suspect's intentions and state of mind was therefore introduced.

In response to the Committee's recommendations, the hitherto complex English law of blackmail was considerably simplified: the underlying basic principle was that the law should be preoccupied primarily with 'the worst cases that ought to be blackmail'.[33] Unlike the Larceny Act 1916, the Theft Act 1968 provided what was described as 'a new code of criminal dishonesty'.[34] Moving the second reading of the preparatory Theft Bill, Lord Stonham drew the attention of the Lords to the creation of the new criminal offence of 'blackmail'. He was, he said, astonished that there was at present no offence called 'blackmail', it was a detestable and cruel offence, 'and it seemed to the Committee, as it does to the Government, that a general maximum penalty of fourteen years was not excessive to cater for the worst cases'.[35] Under the new simplified law the now traditional wider meaning of 'menaces' was retained to cover a host of possible threats. Criminal threats were distinguished from non-criminal threats in terms of the test of subjectivity, and Section 21 of the Act specified three dimensions of criminality:
(1) The defendant must make a 'demand with menaces'.

17

(2) The demand with menaces must be 'unwarranted'. It will be unwarranted unless the defendant makes it 'in the belief — (a) that he has reasonable grounds for making the demand; and (b) that the use of the menaces is a proper means of reinforcing the demands'.

(3) The defendant must make the demand 'with a view to gain for himself or another or with intent to cause loss to another'.[36] In determining the existence of the new offence of 'blackmail' the courts would be expected to search for evidence of criminal intent: in the words of Elyston Morgan, Under Secretary of State at the Home office, 'it seemed wrong to the [Criminal Law Revision] Committee that a person could be guilty of an offence in cases where he honestly believed his conduct to be justified'.[37] Hopefully, evidence pointing to the presence of criminal intent would enable the courts to separate out 'the worst cases' from other presumably less provocative activities. Thus a limited number of *detectable actions*, apparently amenable to direct imputations of criminality, had been formally selected by legislators as the only useful administrative response to the wider moral question of the nature and sources of blackmailing social relations in the modern world.

The 'blackmail menace'

Within the law courts, the committee rooms, Parliament, and the Lords, the gradual criminalisation of blackmail complemented a wider feeling that the fabric of society was under attack from a new direction. Expression of public disquiet achieved its high-point during the 1920s and 1930s: 'By far the most disturbing factor in the crime records of this century'. wrote ex-Detective Inspector Herbert T. Fitch in 1933, 'is the spread of blackmail'.[38]

In 1924 six men were tried at the Old Bailey for attempting to obtain money with menaces, a scheme of systematic blackmail practised on publicans and shopkeepers. The police stated that one of the defendants, a miner, had written to Scotland Yard in 1918, when still in the army and quartered in London, giving details of a system of blackmail in public houses. A man wearing military uniform would enter a pub and some time later two others, pretending to be detectives appeared on the scene. As the publican had served a man in military uniform he was, they informed him, liable to a fine of £100; a small sum paid on the spot would obviate the embarrassment and inconvenience of a court appearance. In some cases as much as £50 was demanded.

The helpful correspondent, said the police, was the man who paid the soldier; although he had given this particular game away his accomplices could not be identified and therefore no action was taken.

The writer excused himself on the grounds that it was merely a drunken carouse and he had been acquitted by a court martial. After this disclosure of past crime, Inspector Bradley was questioned by the Judge:

Mr Justice McCardie:	'There seems to be more blackmail now than there was? '
Inspector Bradley:	'Yes it is very prevalent'.
Mr Justice McCardie:	'It is very difficult to detect because of reluctance of the victim to give his name to the police? '
Inspector Bradley:	'Yes'

Police evidence and the comments of the Judge on this case reveal some preoccupation with a perceived increase in blackmail offences involving both threats against reputation and physical threats; not to mention the two combined in various measures. Passing sentence on the six men, Mr Justice McCardie spelt out the integral characteristics of 'true blackmail':[39]

Civilisation has many cancers, and in my view one of the worst of those cancers is this offence of blackmail. It is a most cruel, callous, and most cowardly offence . . . The result of this blackmail is to inflict slow death on the victim, the object being to extract from his terror as much or more money than he can possibly afford . . . In my view this offence is on the increase. The time has come when, even if men are convicted for the first time of that offence, the Judge should inflict severe punishment. The parks and streets must be made safe, blackmail must be stamped out.

It is not always clear from an overview of contemporary judicial and press comments whether the concept of the blackmail menace, in the 1920s and 1930s, applied specifically to a perceived increase in reputational blackmail, or to an increase in extortion generally. Neither are the experiential sources of definitions of blackmail as 'the cancer of modern society' always clear. Mr Justice McCardie was obviously referring to offences enacted in public places, but sufficient additional recorded comment is available throughout the period to indicate a greater concern over the existence of reputational blackmail than the bare criminal statistics would seem to warrant. 'The Police Journal' published a review of 'recent judicial decisions' on blackmail in 1931 where it observed that threats to disclose discreditable information unless given payment were 'a serious and growing mischief in modern civilisation'.[40] The refusal to give the 'service' of withholding information without some financial consideration had come to be seen as a particular scourge of society. Years afterwards, Sir Travers Humphreys, who appeared in several blackmail prosecutions, wrote that during the 1920s sentences on blackmailers were too lenient, 'whilst the police were in complete agreement with me that this most detestable of crimes was on the increase'.[41]

Normally accessible statistical records provide us with little public information concerning the incidence and characteristics of blackmail. None the less, in what is one of the few criminological references to the incidence of blackmail I have encountered,[42] Hermann Manheim's 'Social Aspects of Crime in England Between the Wars',[43] there is a statement to the effect that the number of prosecutions increased from around 1924, though the annual averages cited refer only to 'Extortion by threats other than threats to accuse'. The 'Criminal Statistics (England and Wales)' include the following annual averages of blackmail offences known to the police:

1920 - 4 : 38
1925 - 9 : 64
1930 - 4 : 91
1935 - 9 : 93

But these particular figures comprise two significantly separate categories, corresponding respectively with Sections 29 and 30 of the Larceny Act 1916: 'Extortion by threats to accuse of crime' and 'Extortion by other threats'. Since these two groups cover a wide variety of threats we are officially left in the dark as to the particular kinds of accusation those worried about the blackmail 'menace' found so unsettling. Up to 1955 the statistics do show that offences labelled 'Extortion by threats to accuse of crime' amounted to a much smaller proportion of the calculated average than those in the second category, which also included physical threats. But in 1955 this dual recording procedure was modified in the statistics, when its replacement with the single category 'Blackmail' (over ten years before the legal ratification of the term), effectively blotted out a marginally more helpful index.[44]

How does this flimsy statistical evidence match up with the notion of the 'blackmail menace' prevalent throughout the inter-war years? Two further clues from court and police practice remain, signifying an awareness of the increasing possibility of blackmail in everyday life:

(1) The conceptualisation of blackmail as 'moral murder'.

(2) An informal undertaking by the courts and the police to preserve the anonymity of any victim prepared to publicly prosecute a blackmailer.

(1)   'Moral murder'

Not long ago two men went to prison for threatening a third with violence if he did not pay them money; they were guilty, said the Recorder of Quarter Sessions, of 'the murder of another man's peace of mind'. 'Moral murder' essentially involves the imputed destruction of another's sense of personal equilibrium through the inducement of fear; the power of the blackmailer consists of the power to frighten the victim into paying up. During the inter-war years this phrase apparently passed into popular usage in the criminal courts and elsewhere when it was specifically drawn upon to stigmatise those who attempted to commercialise the reputations of others, whom they assumed were more vulnerable than themselves. Not only was 'blackmail' a hideous word for a hideous offence, it increasingly came to be used to refer to the vulnerability of public reputation.

Notions of the vulnerability of the victim are particularly important for an appreciation of the willingness of the prosecution to apply the concept of 'moral murder' during court proceedings. Coupling blackmail with criminal libel, S.T. Felstead, spelled out this interpretation of the wider social significance of reputational blackmail: 'Almost invariably, it is a cowardly attack which leaves the victim of it comparatively helpless, because even though he may succeed in having the offender arrested, or alternatively bring an action for damages, some of the mud which has been thrown usually sticks'.[45] The term 'moral murder' dramatises the fear-ridden state induced in the victim by the blackmailer: a public reaction which mirrors the victim's anxiety for the status of his public reputation. The following rather dramatic case, apparently leading to attempted suicide,[46] provides an appropriate illustration:

Case 1 ('moral murder')   The case for the prosecution was that a farm labourer accosted the victim, 'Mr X', in the street saying he was out of work. 'Mr X' took him home and gave him food. The defendant asked if there was anyone else in the house and went upstairs to have a look, 'Mr X' protested, and then the defendant was alleged to have said, 'If you don't give me some money I shall make out a serious charge against you. I am a police constable, and I shall tell the police that you have assaulted me'. It was then stated that 'Mr X' made six or seven payments over about five weeks, totalling £510. He was subsequently found suffering from coal gas poisoning and apparently very nearly lost his life.

Passing sentence of seven years penal servitude, Mr Justice Rowlatt observed that the defendant had:[47]

pleaded guilty to one of the most terrible crimes that could be committed. It could not be too well known that though a man was the blackest criminal, to threaten him with exposure to get money was an abominable crime. [The defendant's] case was to be differentiated from the case of a professional blackmailer . . . [the defendant] was a humble man, not very well instructed, and there was no suggestion that he was a professional blackmailer .

But every honest man in this country, be he prince or labourer, must know what a devilish thing it is to threaten a man with an accusation of crime in order to extort money from him.

Blackmail, as 'moral murder', received a final dramatic touch reflecting the extended significance of money in our society when it was tricked out with the imagery of vampirism and blood-letting. Bleeding a person dry of his resources — a characteristic feature of the criminal stereotype of the blackmailer — became a constant theme associated with the offence of demanding money with menaces. Such ennervating and relentless pressure allegedly produced a state of suicidal despair in response to jeopardised reputation and reduced life chances and cash payments over a period of time were compared with the slow draining away of life blood: a nice indication of the cash register society.

(2)   Confidentiality and preservation of the anonymity of the victim

It is widely believed that blackmail is a hidden offence, buried in secrecy — part of the concealed cost of modern living. Addressing victims of blackmail everywhere, Sir Melville L. Macnaughten wrote in 1914 that if any of:[48]

'these persecuted beings would visit my able successor at the Yard, or any other discreet and learned person in the Criminal Investigation Department, they would be given advice, 'free gratis and for nothing', and in certain cases would be referred to reliable ex-detective officers, who would find a way for them out of their troubles'.

Naturally, the police were in a dilemma since, as they admitted occasionally in court and elsewhere, they had great difficulty in apprehending blackmailers if victims were not willing to denounce those who threatened moral murder. Faced with the task of suppressing the blackmail 'menace' they were not slow in giving assurances that the names of those willing to come forward and denounce their persecutors would be protected and their confidences respected:[49]

'The police are human, they are sympathetic, they are discreet, and their advice is valuable. Those who are being blackmailed or

threatened with such unrighteous demands should take their courage
in hand and consult the Chief Officer of the Police Department in
the district in which they reside. To do so does not necessarily mean
police exposure.'

Members of the judiciary too, made frequent statements in court
urging people who were being blackmailed or threatened with blackmail
to go to the police. After all, by going to the police it was possible to
stave off the appalling effects of moral murder: 'If the prosecutor', stated
the Recorder at the Old Bailey, 'against whom not a word could be said,
had not had the courage to go to the police he might as well have cut
his throat, he would have been bled and bled and bled'.[50] Readers of
textbooks on criminal law know that amongst descriptions and analyses
of the law of blackmail, passages such as the following are not uncommon:
'In such cases it has universally been allowed of late that the prosecutor
should, for the purpose of the trial, be anonymous'.[51] It must be
stressed that this indulgence has never been formally embodied in law
— it began as an informal and negotiable means of encouraging the
prosecution of blackmailers — particular emphasis was laid upon this
consideration for those victims willing to go to the police from the very
early 1920s. Thus a brief report in 'The Times' of 15 June 1921 was
headlined: 'Blackmailed Man's Name Withheld'. The prosecutor's name
was not disclosed 'but it was stated that he was a businessman of good
standing in the city'. Otherwise very little detail was provided in this
brief record of events at Liverpool Assizes, except that the victim said
that blackmail had been going on over several years, and he had parted
with a considerable sum of money 'in order to save his name'.[52]
    It has proved difficult to locate any exact point at which the
traditional willingness to offer the protection of anonymity to the
victim during a criminal prosecution of blackmail began. Whilst being
of particular relevance to us here, such offers of protection are not, of
course, confined to blackmail proceedings. What can be stated with
certainty is that from this point — 1921 — through to the later 1930s,
statements by judges, affirming protection and exhorting victimised
members of the public to come forward, were relatively frequently
reported. In the words then, of Sir Ernest Wilde, K.C., consigning a
window cleaner and his wife to gaol: 'they had been convicted on the
clearest evidence of the foul offence of blackmail — a prevalent
offence which was being stamped out by proper judicial severity. It
was because names were suppressed that people had the courage to
come forward and prosecute'.[53]
    All of which is not to suggest that such offers no longer occur or that
negotiated concealment by the authorities is no longer considered
necessary; the point is that the particular emphasis given to the initiation

of this informal policy, in the years following the First World War, reflected an enhanced consciousness of blackmail inherited from the nineteenth century. 'I do not want it thought', stated counsel for the prosecution at the Old Bailey in 1936, 'that the doctor has anything to hide, but it is customary in these Courts that anyone prosecuting in these sorts of cases should not have his or her name disclosed, because it always causes a great deal of unpleasant publicity'.[54]

Chapter 2

'True Blackmail'

Reputation: what others are not thinking about you.
Tom Masson

Underpinning the legal recognition of the criminality of blackmail lay the assumption that it was a social evil — a parasitical growth on the otherwise healthy body of society, sapping its strength and undermining its constitution. J.K. Ferrier, whom we have met already, told his readers that 'of all the forms of crime, blackmailing is surely the most vicious, vile and villainous; it is even lower and more contemptible than cheating at cards'.[1]

In 1874 a scandal in the USA brought to light a 'widespread system' of blackmail in several of the main cities. In the words of the 'New York Times', the 'evil has been growing rapidly for many years, until the practice of extorting money from nervous people by threats would appear to have become almost a recognised profession'.[2] The case was cited of a 'distinguished member of the American Bar' who paid blackmail for fifteen years to keep secret an offence of which he was entirely innocent. Reporting these unsettling events, 'The Times' (London) noted that blackmail in the USA had assumed two distinctive shapes: discharged clerks threatening to divulge the business secrets of their late employers, and what were called discharged 'subordinates' in public or private offices, threatening their late superiors with personal attacks in the daily press. Of course, said 'The Times', only the 'lower class of journals' would lend themselves to dishonourable practices of this nature; 'respectable newspapers' could be relied upon not to participate.

Clearly, all was not well on the other side of the Atlantic; we in Britain could, however, still afford to congratulate ourselves upon our economic moderation and good sense.[3]

'Until better taste prevails, all public men in the United States will
be exposed to the chance of having their good names defiled by
scandalous calumnies wherever they happen to give offence to some
unscrupulous subordinate. Perhaps this evil state of things may be
one of the products of the marvellous prosperity about which
Americans are so fond of boasting. If so, the more moderate growth
of wealth in the United Kingdom may not be without some advantage.

'The Times' was not slow to fall back on a partial form of economic
determinism to explain disturbances in hierarchical social relationships
overseas; undue reliance could not be placed on the pursuit of wealth to
produce a wholly harmonious society. Blackmail offences were
undoubtedly acted out against an economic backcloth; ultimately,
however, the origins of this new social problem could only be traced to
the presence of certain 'unscrupulous', and worse, 'subordinate'
individuals, who just weren't prepared to play the game.

Victorian victims of blackmail were by no means always socially
prominent, though for the most part the ones who appeared in court
proved to be representative of the advantaged classes. In 1897, Earl
Carrington pursued a 'well dressed middle aged woman' to the courts
after she had sent him a series of demanding letters, written she later
claimed, under the mistaken impression he was a 'Mr Lloyd' with whom
she had associated for twenty years. After abandoning her claim to
£200 compensation for a broken relationship, and changing her plea to
guilty of demanding money with menaces, the prisoner heard Mr Justice
Darling outline the establishment reaction to evidence of blackmail:[4]

It was [he stated] the misfortune of persons occupying a prominent
position, socially or politically, that they were easily made the target
of attacks such as these. It was not everyone who had the courage to
come into court and show the absolute falsehood of the accusation
made; but Earl Carrington had done that, and he had performed a
great service to the public in so doing.

Amidst the rapid growth of a commercialised way of life, the British
law of blackmail took shape as an instrument for safeguarding the
reputations of individual citizens against the potentially exploitative
activities of a defineable criminal minority. During the latter part of the
nineteenth, and the first quarter of the present century, the growth of
free enterprise company promotions produced a number of prosecutions
specifically involving what was called 'financial journalism'. Company
promoters anxious to attract potential shareholders necessarily relied
upon a respectable reputation for success.[5] People who had money to

invest in the new companies turned to the pages of the proliferating financial journals for advice as to the most reliable men in the market. By printing an article unfavourable to a particular businessman — an attack on his character or his business acumen — a competitor could perhaps benefit himself, if he was a rival promoter, or collect a profit by agreeing not to publish a discrediting article in the future. Blackmail of this variety was attempted by the proprietor of a paper with the title 'Financial Whose Who', proclaimed the official organ of the 'Investors Protection and Information Agency', in 1897.

The prosecutor was the promoter of the British Bechuanaland Gold and Diamond Fields Limited. An article had been published in the 'Financial Whose Who' to the effect that the paper was about to print a story concerning a man later identified as the victim, and that if it became known he was connected with a company his investors would desert him. An agreement had been drawn up, it was stated, between the prosecutor and the two defendants transferring to them cash and shares in consideration of an undertaking not to publish the sensitive articles in question.[6]

Two years later, after a separate incident, two men were indicted at the Old Bailey for 'threatening to publish matters and things of and concerning' an auctioneer, with a view to extorting money. The accused had offered to keep an article unfavourable to the victim out of a financial newspaper for a fee of £5. Having made sure that the article had actually been typed and after having paid over the £5, the auctioneer reported both of the accused, who denied his allegations, to the police. One of the men was found not guilty and discharged, the second received twelve months' imprisonment with hard labour.[7]

Birmingham Assizes in 1912 witnessed the conviction of 'an agent', who received three years penal servitude for sending letters demanding money with menaces, to the general manager of the Prudential Assurance Company. In these letters the defendant proposed to abstain from publishing matters relating to the company. Prosecuting counsel stated that prior to these events a series of articles had appeared in 'John Bull' attacking the methods and stability of the Company. It was announced the defendant had taken advantage of this situation to write posing as a disinterested friend, both of the company and the person who had written the original articles, offering to save the firm from further attack. In the first letter to the company he stated 'If you deem it desirable to make any effort to stop any further supply of articles from this source I will intimate your wish and approach Bottomley's contributor and write you again'. Evidence revealed the accused had written one article for 'John Bull' signed 'Black Sheep', which had been printed and paid for, and another article which was unpublished. Apparently, as the negotiations proceeded, the defendant dropped the pretence of go-between and eventually met the manager of the company in the role of an actual contributor. At this meeting he had agreed not to write any more articles, if he received £20. In court the accused denied he had intended to pressurise the Prudential Company: 'He meant it to be inferred that he had journalistic abilities which were for sale and that he would write as well for the Company as against them'.[8]

Legitimate and fraudulent businessmen alike were vulnerable at this stage in the growth of capitalism. Late in the 1920s the writer J.C. Ellis summarised this phase in our socio-economic history:[9]

> The printer without a conscience and without scruple who is prepared to do anything for money on the condition that his name and address are not attached to the sheet, pamphlet or book, makes a very effective partner for a certain kind of blackmailer. At one time there were nearly a score of them in and around London, and during the golden era of the fraudulent company promoter they were kept busy by shady clients who were profiting by their knowledge of the so-called financiers.

Accessibility to a cheap printing plant and the possession of confidential inside information on the lives of honest and dishonest city men, Ellis argued, facilitated the emergence and brief flourishing of this specific method of making a living.

Basil Tozer agrees with Ellis that 'Newspaper blackmail' went into a decline during the inter-war years: 'This sort of thing still goes on but is less common than in pre-war days. The penalties imposed on convicted blackmailers have become so severe that those who at one time practised blackmail of this sort with comparative impunity now think two or three times before running the risk of arrest'.[10] The point is that legal prescription and actual prosecutions followed in the wake of public awareness that this kind of offensive activity was taking place in the community.

The connection between blackmail and journalism was not limited to the financial press. An early exponent offering advice on stocks and shares, together with comment on the relative integrity of various company promotors, was the famous MP and wit, Henry Labouchère. Invited to contribute to a newspaper, 'The World', which first appeared in 1874, he offered to write a series of city articles exposing swindling company-promoters and other unreliable businessmen 'in a manner that was entirely fresh to journalism and extremely obnoxious to many fellow-journalists'. He set out to show the world, writes his biographer Hesketh Pearson, that the respectable section of the population was not exempt from its quota of reprehensible bloodsuckers. Intent on his crusade, a few years later Labouchère established his own journal, 'Truth': 'Blackmailers, imposters, baby-farmers, wife-beaters, bogus business-men, hypocrites, cheats and charlatans of every description were exposed by him; and, whenever they thought there was a chance of damages, the exposure was invariably followed by a legal action'. Not surprisingly, throughout the latter years of the nineteenth century, he made notable appearances in law courts answering charges of libel.[11]

After Labouchère's death in 1912, 'The Times' reported that the founders of 'The World' were the originators of 'personal journalism', which, Andy Logan has noted, comprised 'gossipy reports of life among the upper classes, laced with intimate trivia and revelation of indiscretion'. Labouchère and his collaborator, Edmund Yates, were described as pioneers of British society journalism, having engineered for the first time in history a mass invasion of the privacy of the privileged classes and 'set us all listening at the keyhole'.[12]

The deceased, we need hardly add, would not have agreed with this verdict. As a radical MP he saw himself working towards democracy; making one contribution towards the removal of traditional barriers between the classes. What Labouchère's efforts did prove was that investigative journalism, probing the concealed lives of well placed people, could act as an unsettling force in social life — whatever its motives. Aleister Crowley, the notorious practitioner of black magic, was one who in his younger days, reflected the new sensitivity over news and reputation. Smarting from attacks upon himself and his occult ceremonies in 'John Bull', Crowley made a significant distinction between honourable and dishonourable journalism relevant to the popular belief in the parasitical nature of blackmail. The 'better class newspapers and magazines', he noted in his 'Confessions', produced articles containing sympathetic and 'laudatory criticisms of the most encouraging kind', about his activities, but unfortunately there was 'another side of London life which till that time I had hardly suspected: that certain newspapers rely for their income upon blackmail'. Disreputable papers flourished, added Crowley with heavy irony, because they were on the receiving end of the support of 'a large class of people' in England; who 'argue from their own personal experience that wherever human beings happen to be together in a subdued light they can have no idea in their minds but that of indecent assault'.[13] Some people, it seemed, were only too ready to assume occult ceremonies cloaked a wide array of blackmailable sexual perversions.[14]

On a somewhat higher plane, it was generally conceded that journalism — a new and powerful social force — had its responsibilities; and one of those responsibilities was a refusal to traffick, solely on the basis of commercial gain, in discreditable information. Above all, honourable factual reporting involved the exercise of restraint over the publication of such information, unless it could be shown to be in the 'public interest'. 'Straight' journalism — objective factual reportage — was compared favourably with the concoction of the 'human interest' story, by implication fabricated from the skilled distortion of selective biographical 'facts', in the interests of enhanced circulation.[15]

Overall, the increasing publicity given to more systematic methods of collecting and transmitting biographical data, contributed to a new awareness that social change had undoubtedly increased the potential of the blackmailer. Basil Tozer, for instance, expressed disquiet over the soaring popularity of psychoanalysis in the 1920s: one consequence was, he argued, a growth in the number of unscrupulous people opening clinics for those suffering from nervous problems. Tozer alleged that many of the patients were the victims of 'neurasthenia which came frequently from indulgence in certain forms of vice, or from general dissipation'. An opening for blackmail was thus created from this conjunction of perversity and therapy: 'Before the first sitting had ended the patient generally described events in her past life which, under normal conditions, nothing would have induced her to speak about'.[16] (Significantly, the patient is female in this particular version of the struggle between the weak-willed, and the strong.) Note too, the blackmailer is unscrupulously stong-minded and skilful in extracting guilty secrets to sell back to the weak-willed victim.

Victorian rules for divorce, reflecting an iniquitous double standard of morality, [17] serve as a further interesting example of this tortured theme. The Divorce Act of 1857 provided an opportunity for the collection and publication of titillatory news items, culled from the lives of those wealthy enough to apply for a legal end to their marriage, which only the advent of a more 'permissive'[18] approach to sexuality and marital breakdown has diminished. The stimulation of 'human interest' was, of course, part and parcel of the overall disapproval of divorce which is slowly ceasing to bedevil us. Apart from encouraging the profession of private detection,[19] it created a flourishing market for divorce court reportage. In other words, scandalous news, potentially damaging to the reputations of those immediately involved derived its peculiarly diverting flavour from the provision in the divorce act that a man need only prove one adulterous liaison to get a divorce, whereas a woman had to show her husband guilty of adultery together with another injury such as bigamy, cruelty, incest, rape, unnatural acts, or desertion. So great was the tide of public interest, the 'Saturday Review' noted in 1864, that:[20]

unsavoury reports of the Divorce Court, the disgusting details of harlotry and vice, the filthy and nauseous annals of the brothel, the prurient letters of adulterers and adulteresses, the modes in which intrigues may be carried out, the diaries and meditations of married sinners, these are now part of our domestic life.

For an indication of the kind of coverage allotted to divorce cases, it is is worth turning to Frank Harris who went to court to hear the divorce proceedings between Lord and Lady Colin Campbell in 1886. The case, Harris writes, was full of the 'most scabrous details' and he promised his readers to give 'the fullest account possible of the trial'. The question was really 'how far I should report the lady's revelations'.[21]

The case lasted for nineteen days and led, towards the end of the same year, to Lord Colin Campbell's appearance at Westminster Police Court to give evidence against a 'well dressed' clerk, who had written him the following letter:[22]

Dec. 1, 1886. My dear Lord —
Unless you send £100 before Friday 7 pm to below address I shall communicate something to Sir Charles Russell which will surprise him, and the result of which will surprise you. Money in Bank of England notes must be there by Friday. It will be of no use to send before to try and take proceedings against me as I shall not be there.
Yours
M.D.D.
PS If you want to win your case, my evidence had best be unheard. Take the hint.

Sir Charles Russell was counsel for Lady Colin Campbell, and the letter is clearly an offer not to reveal information prejudicial to her husband's case. As it turned out this prosecution for attempted blackmail revealed that the writer, subsequently committed for trial at the Old Bailey, was not acquainted with either of the two parties, nor did he have any sensitive biographical details to withhold. Although this attempt was ultimately summed up as 'the foolish freak of a young man of 19', and Lord Colin Campbell himself recommended mercy, 'The Times' reported the judge's opinion that:[23]

Lord Colin Campbell was well advised in instituting this prosecution. Having regard to what was taking place at the time the letter was written, he thought it imperative that Lord Colin Campbell, as a man of honour, should institute these proceedings against the defendant, and Lord Colin was now dealing with him with considerable mercy and leniency.

Several years later, on 24 April, 1923, Lord Balfour of Burleigh questioned Viscount Buckmaster as to whether the attention of the government had been drawn to suggestions that certain sections of the press had given undue publicity to indecent details in some law cases. The wrongdoer, Viscount Buckmaster replied, was unlikely to be deterred by the possibility that his misdeeds may be published to the world:[24]

> It is not merely that you are going to interfere with the wrongdoer. You are going to pillory the person who has not done wrong, and that, to my mind, is the great scandal connected with these reports. A woman who has done no wrong at all has to go to the court to disclose in public matters as to which she would rather die of shame than mention them in public. She has to give her evidence before a court that is crowded with vulgar, idle sightseers, who have not gathered for the purpose of seeing justice administered — if they wanted to see justice administered they could go to the Admiralty Court — but who have gathered for the purpose of hearing of unclean matters from the lips of a woman. And to make a woman who is seeking for rights which exist, and which the laws of this country still give her, go through that torture before she can obtain them is to do something which offends the most elementary principles of justice.

Concomitantly 'respectable' morality, the advent of literacy, and technical improvements in all modes of communication, had multiplied the avenues along which blackmail negotiations could proceed. Dismissed from the service of an army major at Hastings, in 1898, and having unsuccessfully applied to his employer for a character reference, money, and clothes, a butler finally posted a series of letters, one of which read:[25]

> you know money is what I want, so I have done. If you do not get by tomorrow £50 for me — by loan or whatever you like — I shall put the case before your father and the 'Daily Telegraph'. There is no nonsense about this . . . you can clear the country, for I swear I will do what I say, if only to ruin you . . . £1 is no use now.

The commercialisation of biographical material depended upon the publication of reputational information for profit;[26] pioneers of mass circulation newspapers were quick to realise that 'no popular journal could succeed and maintain its position without getting itself talked about and without constantly changing and improving its contents'.[27] A selective process was at work whereby the cultivation of the 'popular appetite for scandal' materially assisted sales. These processes fostered their own validation — profitable audience reaction.[28]

The idea persisted that a depraved minority, attaching themselves parasitically to the system and growing fat on the misfortunes of their betters, could be identified and controlled, leaving society as a whole in a balanced state of health. Acknowledging that blackmail was an unsightly business, the law set itself the task of prescribing the *general iniquity* of 'demanding money with menaces'; providing at the same time sufficient latitude for courtroom dispute over the *specific events* constituting a particular offence.

Thus, the criminal law retained two basic functions. First, it ratified the commercialisation of society, formally setting out the main rules purporting to regulate business practice — a sort of code of honour defining legitimate procedures for the exchange of cash, goods, and services.[29] Second, it acted as a vehicle for pronouncements concerning the kinds of relationship into which the principles of business should not intrude.[30]

> Women must know, and be made to understand [stated a judge in the 1930s] that if as you say happened in this case, a man is intimate with them there is no reason why they should blackmail him in years to come. You have admitted writing to him with the intention of getting money from him. You were attempting to get it from him by threatening to let people know that which was a secret between the two of you.

One implication of the whole process of blackmail prosecution since the 1850s has been that certain relationships must be protected because they generate information bearing some market value for all concerned. Reputations, after all, are the product of group activity and some relationships are vulnerable because they temptingly expose members to inside information which is not normally accessible. Consequently they may be labelled 'private and confidential':[31] cloaked in secrecy and hedged by rules, including when evoked, the occasional protection of the criminal law. Living in the Watergate era we are all fully aware of the strategic nature of confidential relationships, wherein sensitive reputational information is generated, and not infrequently, selectively edited for public consumption.

The stereotype of blackmail

Against this historical backcloth of rapid technical and economic change, any understanding of a given act of blackmail and the subsequent prosecution of a transaction, must arise out of our appreciation of the various motives which the blackmailer, the victim, subsequent participants, and any witnesses, consider meaningful for the initiation and development of the interchange. Such understanding is directly dependent upon the quality of information available to us, yet with the exception of police and legal memoirs, it is almost as difficult to find fully documented incidents in books, the press, and other records as it is to locate and investigate actual transactions.[32]

Police investigations occasionally yield unambiguous evidence of blackmailing when the search for a solution to some other crime is in progress. Sometimes, too, civil proceedings reveal an unsavoury undercurrent: at the Old Bailey in March 1938, a woman pleaded to a bigamous marriage which had come to light when her putative husband pressed for a divorce. In court the defendant said she left the man in question because she was being blackmailed; apparently she had used money provided by her bigamous husband for the rent, to seal the lips of a blackmailer.[33]

Some commentators have assumed that blackmail lies at the heart of many unsolved crimes.

> If it were possible to write a complete history of London's blackmailing gangs [wrote J.C. Ellis] a solution would be found for many crimes... and among them would be at least two murders. For blackmail is often the root from which crimes grow and ten years and more may elapse before the offshoot comes to maturity. And it is the impossibility of tracing it back to its real origin which compels the police to admit themselves beaten.

Later, Ellis observed:[34]

> if we were to run through the records of the courts since the beginning of the century we should be surprised by the almost unbelievably small number of blackmailers who have been brought to book. And those who have been exposed and punished are for the most part unrepresentative of this highly specialised form of crime.

Consequently, published sources tend not only to be highly selective in the crimes they report but also concentrate on considerably oversimplified versions of what has taken place. A fully-rounded account, presenting the views of all participants in the transaction, hardly ever appears. Quoted in full from 'The Times' of 3 December 1897, the following example can be taken as illustrative of the restrained nature of many trial reports:

> William Henry Banks, 33, labourer, was charged with feloniously accusing John Englefield of an infamous crime, with intent to extort money, at Scarborough, on August 19. Mr H. Gawan Taylor

prosecuted. The prisoner not being represented by counsel, whilst Mr Nield held a watching brief on behalf of an interested party. In the result the foreman of the jury, after some deliberation on their part, said: 'The jury have come to the conclusion that the prisoner is guilty of the charge, but that there is not sufficient evidence to prove it'. This announcement was received with loud laughter. The learned Judge said to the jury: 'That is in law a verdict of not guilty, and if it is any satisfaction to you I agree with the sense of your verdict'. The prisoner was then discharged.

Proceedings which have caused a great deal of social furore (for instance, the rather unusual Chrimes case of mass blackmailing detailed in Chapter 5), receive a lengthier treatment than the more commonplace cases. But for the most part, the available accounts reveal much more about how it is generally considered people ought to behave — in other words the *prescribed legitimate reaction* to news of a defined offence of blackmail — than about why blackmail is possible, or how much of it is 'really' going on. The menace of blackmail remains an unknown menace — even to the police —[35] and the full enormity of the offence can only be appreciated when concrete instances are revealed to the authorities and passed into the criminal courts for the edification of the public. In this situation of ambiguity and doubt, so accurately reflected in academic debates over the precise legal status of blackmail, a stereotype of blackmail, encapsulating all its potentially destructive features, has become essential.[36]

Stereotypes are images of reality; in the sense used here, they are the amalgamation of signs and symbols we feed into disturbing situations in order to interpret their meaning, and as a guide to appropriate action. They help to reduce complex events to manageable proportions,[37] but they may be misleading in that they oversimplify reality by failing to take all perspectives into account. The stereotyping of blackmail requires the construction of a formalised model which can be regularly employed to allocate its various manifestations into a series of conventional categories — a sort of social straitjacketing. Andy Logan has provided a colourful instance of this process in his pen portrait of D'Alton Mann:[38]

Although Colonel William D'Alton Mann, for nearly thirty years the publisher of a New York Magazine called 'Town Topics', has been described as the ranking blackmailer of American society, he was nothing like the stereotype of his undercover trade, the sly, skulking figure with the mirthless smile who exacts his tribute in some shadowy rendezvous . . . the Colonel bore a striking resemblance to a Saint — rather than Old Nick. 'A rousing, bouncing, noisy, vigorous, open-hearted, choleric old man', was the way one of his editorial employees of the time described him, adding, 'What wonder that everybody loved him? '.

The full sterotype of blackmail is double-edged. It refers to both *the act of blackmail* and to the *character of the blackmailer*, who is invested with an initiatory role. On hand to describe the actual offence, in its 'ideal' form, is the concept of 'true blackmail', more popularly known as 'moral murder' by means of threatened character assassination. Although true blackmail is not a legal term, it has frequently been incorporated with enterprise of crime and punishment when determining whether interaction between the main parties in a prosecution can effectively be labelled 'blackmail' or whether it ought to be called something else. True blackmail represents the socially approved theory about what is supposed to happen when one person blackmails another: a summary of the stages through which *any* blackmail transaction will predictably pass once the victim has submitted to the first demand. It offers insight into the tortured state of mind enveloping those victims whose fate has come to the attention of the authorities; an awful warning of the dangers surrounding us in society.

Character assassination differs from moral murder in so far as it refers to the *instrument* of blackmail: the visible destruction of life chances, regardless of the victim's state of mind. The possibility that such destruction will actually occur, if the blackmailer reveals his information, is of course dependent on a variety of social factors, some of which we shall explore later. For the moment, a valuable point of comparison is the foreclosure of Oscar Wilde's glittering career at the end of the last century. Wilde was prosecuted under Clause 9 of the Criminal Law Amendement Act 1885,[39] after he had brought an unsuccessful libel action against the Marquess of Queensberry, who accused him of being a 'sodomite'. His first trial for homosexual offences started at the Old Bailey on 26 April 1895; the jury failed to agree to a verdict and a new trial began on 20 May, ending on the 25th with a sentence of two years' imprisonment with hard labour.[40] Imprisonment brought Wilde material ruin: he lost his income, his possessions, and his family; and his name became synonymous with effete homosexual perversion. Following the widespread newspaper coverage of all the trials, children playing in the streets quickly learned to call out 'Oscar Wilde' after any passing male apparently overdressed or effeminate.[41]

Not only was his reputation as an author temporarily shattered as a result of the prosecution; the publication of Wilde's particular sexual interests transformed him into a stereotypical deviant and his name was used to stigmatise a whole assortment of other men who happened to have some sort of feeling for homosexuality and quite a few who did not.

Case II ('Oscar Wilde business')   On 7 May 1895 at Marlborough Street police court in London a hairdresser recalled that he went into a lavatory in Oxford Market, London and coming out was accosted by a youth of about 17. The following series of incidents were then unfolded to readers of 'The Times':

The Youth	'Can you give me a drink please Sir?'
Hairdresser	'A drink boy! Why should I treat you, where do you come from?'
The Youth	'I am out of work and hard up'.

The hairdresser said he then attempted to get away from the boy but two men came up and caught him by the arms. They stated they were detectives and were going to take him to the station. He replied 'I will come, but for what I don't know', to which they responded ominously: 'For some Oscar Wilde business'. Turning then to the boy the detectives asked, 'What has he been doing with you in the lavatory?' The boy started to cry and said 'I will give you five shillings to let me go'. Eventually he agreed that the hairdresser had 'something to do with him' in the lavatory. At this point one of the detectives expressed his reluctance to arrest the hairdresser: 'You are a man of position and I should not like to mix you up in this sort of thing'. As they walked along, one man on either side of the hairdresser holding him by the arms, he was asked 'What are you going to do to settle it?' A law-abiding man, the hairdresser replied that he did not want any settlement at all but would go to the police station with them. They then said 'We will make it pretty thick for you, my lord. You had better settle it'.

At that moment the victim realised his captors were not policemen, called two passers-by to his aid and the would-be blackmailers disappeared. They were later arrested and jointly charged with demanding money with menaces.[42]

In spite of his own ordeal, Wilde retained a sense of personal individuality, ending his days courageously in exile; a victim of character assassination of the crudest kind, he did not succumb totally to the effects of moral murder.[43] Ultimately, his identity did not disintegrate nor did all his friends forsake him.

By contrast, the commercial moral of the stereotype of true blackmail is appropriately: 'lose your money and you lose your life'. J.C. Ellis tells the story of a young widow who married the only son and heir of a wealthy baronet. Suddenly, out of the blue, she was given a letter which changed her 'from a beautiful, happy girl of twenty-six, into a haggard woman of forty'. It allegedly came from the husband she believed dead, and brought with it the possibility of an accusation of bigamy. She paid, and in six months was in a pitiable condition: 'Nearly all her jewellery had been pawned and she was talking with a pathetic earnestness of her dislike of wearing precious stones; her banking account was overdrawn and she owed two thousand pounds to a money-lender, while it seemed she had lost her youth and beauty'.[44] Morality tales of this kind abound in the available literature; above all true blackmail is portrayed as an inexorable process which will not cease until the blackmailer is eliminated.

Case III (true blackmail)   What follows is a report from Bristol Assizes of the prosecuting counsel's description of events in the everyday life of a porter, his wife, and the milk roundsman during August 1930.

Mr A, 'a milk roundsman, kissed Mrs B once or twice and told her improper stories. When A called to deliver milk on October 25, Mr B accused him in the presence of Mrs B, her mother, and a lodger, of attempting to seduce Mrs B. A denied it, but Mrs B supported her husband'. Allegedly B then said: 'I shall want £5 damages for that. If you don't pay I'll tell your employer'. A agreed to pay and wrote a letter dictated by B agreeing to pay him £5 at ten shillings a week for 'flirtations with your wife'. The letter was witnessed by the lodger.

On October 30, B made 'graver charges' and A wrote another letter dictated by B attributing his evil misdeeds to drink. Two weeks later B apparently stated his wife had written a confession to his solicitor that A had seduced her and demanded £50. On December 2, B said he had to take his wife to a doctor who had ordered a specialist examination. B had also discovered, it was related by the prosecution, that A had a bank account and demanded £10. A wrote another letter 'referring to the condition of your wife' and paid B £7.

Four days after these events, B discovered A was engaged and made him write out an IOU for £90. It was further alleged that B threatened A with a loaded revolver and also with co-respondent papers. At this point, Mr A summoned the assistance of a solicitor who referred him to the police.[45]

The outstanding feature of the true blackmail stereotype is escalation of the demand until the victim is perceptibly driven to quiet desperation. Obviously a blackmailer will depend upon various cues which he will use as guides to an assessment of the state of wealth of the victim, and his point of least resistance. Victims possessing more ostentatious signs of wealth, of course, are in a more vulnerable position but the main issue is not really the amount of money demanded in absolute terms, but the *proportion* of a victim's income and its relation to other aspects of his life. In terms of proportionate demand, any individual from any social class can become the victim of systematic true blackmail.

Case IV (true blackmail)   Tried at the Old Bailey in 1931, the following prosecution provides a useful comparative illustration of the disastrous consequences incompetent escalation can produce for the blackmailer.

A schoolmaster and a hairdresser at Gravesend pleaded not guilty to demanding money with menaces from 'Mr X', described as 'a man of society'. It was alleged they had stolen compromising photographic negatives, taken at a party, from Mr X's club. The defendant then wrote, reminding him of the existence of the negatives:

You may recollect being photographed 10 months ago at Maidenhead. These photographic negatives, which are in my possession, were to say the least very personal and should be of greatest interest to you. If such is the case you will reply to me, as you might like to regain possession of them.

Mr X refused to involve himself in the proposed transaction and did not reply. In September he received a second letter including a free offer: 'I am enclosing prints from the negatives about which I wrote'. The prosecutor then went to see his solicitor. Early in October he received a third letter: 'Having ignored my previous communications I presume that you have lost interest in your rather indiscreet escapade at Maidenhead'. The writer went on to say that if he did not hear soon he would dispose of them to the best advantage.

There followed a fourth letter suggesting an interview between Mr X and the defendants. Mr X did not take up this offer. By this time the unsuccessful blackmailers were getting desperate. In December a fifth letter appeared stating the writer was going to send a print to each of the 1,300 members of Mr X's club for Christmas (in court it was said the club had a membership of very well known people). Mr X now took legal advice and, under police surveillance, met one of the defendants in Soho, where he was told that the man before him was acting for two people demanding thousands but he would try to 'cook their goose' for £100. Giving evidence in court the police said that the defendant in question had been heard to say he wanted £50 for the negatives.[46]

Because practical police interest in a case is confined to providing the court with a demonstration of technical guilt, evidence of escalated demand is extremely valuable. Since such admissible evidence is not always available in corroborative detail, (blackmail letters may be open to a variety of interpretations) the police often have to channel their efforts into obtaining a first-hand account of a single blackmail transaction so they can bring about a successful prosecution. Accordingly, certain cases of blackmail have provided the police with an opportunity for those dramatic escapades more frequently found in novels: dressing up and posing as victims, hiding in the boots of cars, eavesdropping on telephone conversations, lurking under open windows, standing in cupboards, and loitering in cafés or parks, all to catch a wary blackmailer in the act.

When a solicitor's clerk was charged in the Justice Room at the Guildhall, London, with the attempted blackmailing of a financial agent, an interesting account, revealing the importance of the presence of external witnesses to a blackmail transaction, came to light. Following demands for money from the defendant (unspecified in the report), the financial agent consulted the police, and an inspector and a sergeant arranged to observe a forthcoming meeting between himself and the suspect at the Moorgate station buffet. On this occasion victim and offender entered, ordered drinks, and eventually went to a table and sat down where they were still visible to the policemen concealed behind a small screen. After about an hour the agent passed money across to the defendant who was promptly arrested; when cautioned he apparently agreed the police charge was 'correct and fair'.[47]

Here we have one variant of the 'fair cop' concept. To bring about a 'fair cop' it is necessary for victims, or putative victims, to go to the police and report forthcoming transactions. Initiation of this set of procedures will clearly only take place in certain situations where prior evidence, with regard to the criminality of transactions past or transactions proposed by the alleged blackmailer is inaccessible. In either case the complainant obviously feels secure enough to seek official help. Once concealed from the unknowing suspect, the police are able to record such statements as: 'We are going to have some money from you tonight'.[48] Such evidence makes an important contribution to an effective label of criminality, applied both on arrest and during the trial. The notion of the 'fair cop' indicates concurrence by the offender with the label of criminal intentionality applied by the police. Not all cases of blackmail fall within this category, but they do illustrate an important relationship between the exigencies of police work and the stereotype of true blackmail. In effect most reported cases appear to involve a gradual process of evaluation, whereby an eventual adverse reaction on the victim's part to the proposition before him, is transformed, under police guidance, into a direct imputation of offensive criminality.

One important variation on this theme of the 'fair cop' occurs when the police, at the request of a victim, visit the alleged blackmailer and advise him to restrain his demands. In this instance a series of pressures are brought to bear prior to arrest. Some evidence exists to show that warning tactics tend to be employed when the victim does not wish to prosecute because of some relatively close relationship with the alleged blackmailer. Or, more significantly, when the police or the victim later discover that the blackmailer is some close relation.

As far as the victim's inner state is concerned, true blackmail follows from the successful commercialisation of information about some aspect of his life, regardless of the nature of discreditable information the blackmailer threatens to publicise. Sir Chartres Biron, the famous London magistrate, drew on his years of experience to describe the basic characteristics of true blackmail:[49]

> Some of the most dangerous criminals that come before West End courts are the blackmailers: subtle in method and ruthless in execution, the money they make is inconceivable. Their plan of campaign is simple. A man is selected, with wealth or position, or both if possible. Either they find out something to his discredit, or entrap him into some compromising position which may place him at their mercy. If he happens to be married this is not so difficult. If not more discreditable plans are devised. Once the victim pays to keep them quiet all is well; such a weakness is treated as an admission and used as such. The blackmailer is quite ruthless and his extortion knows no limits.

Because most sources of accessible information on blackmail derive from court proceedings, or at least encounters with the police, their content is organised around the penal stereotype of true blackmail. An assumed explanation is present in this concentration of attention upon what are seen to be the characteristically horrifying consequences to the victim concerned. True blackmail is seen as something which is *done* to the victim, often typically portrayed as passive, and generally more sinned against than sinning. Inevitably such a stereotype facilitates the degradation and punishment of the offender; going well beyond the stark legal category of demanding money with menaces it has five key characteristics:

> (1) it tends to be an urban phenomenon, often found in the big cities which cater for the creation and satisfaction of illicit desires, and harbour the 'criminal classes';
> (2) a long term business designed to provide the blackmailer with an income for a lifetime;
> (3) the victim faces material ruin and eventually suffers psychological collapse;

(4) the victim is powerless in the grip of the blackmailer and will rarely go for help;
(5) victims, or potential victims, may be found in all classes of society but it is the honourable, the respectable and above all the rich, who are the most bedevilled.

Certain features of the blackmail transaction, as revealed in court, do provide some validation of the dramatic imagery investing the stereotype of blackmail:

(1) The idea that some men and women are unduly timid or vulnerable and it is therefore cowardly, unfair, and dishonourable to threaten their reputations is particularly significant. Just as there is an 'ideal type' of blackmail there is also an ideal type of victim. To give one example, in 1921 a builder's merchant of Battersea was said in court to have become the target of attempted blackmail because he was 'easily affected by alcohol owing to neurasthenia contracted during war service'. He had been in Piccadilly late one night under the influence of drink and not wishing to return home to friends, with whom he was staying, in that condition he wanted to find a hotel. During his search he spoke to two men who found him a place and left him. Next morning he discovered his wallet had disappeared and the two defendants —both aged seventeen — later called at his business address and 'threatened to make an accusation against him' if he did not pay £30. The potential victim refused to give anything and said he would charge them with blackmail.[50] In British society, and also the USA, the most frequently discussed ideal type of blackmail victim is the homosexual, largely because homosexuality tends to receive a great deal of adverse publicity, but we should be chary of the idea that homosexuals are the only ideal victims.

(2) Recurring demands for money are usually cited as the cause of a blackmailer's undoing and are a frequent feature in recorded cases, simply because they are one reason why some blackmailers get caught. There are plenty of examples: sometimes blackmail letters will arrive from the same person after a lapse of years — a case was reported not long ago where there was a gap of nearly thirty years between the tailing off of one sequence and the appearance of a second set of demands. Some blackmailers too will sell the names of victims to other blackmailers when they have tired of them and, as the victim sees it, agreed to make no more demands.[51]

Certainly, as I have just indicated, some situations are seen as more productive of potentially discreditable information than others:[52]

It is closely allied with the homosexual, the pervert and the prostitute . . . Strong-willed people frequently report attempts of this nature to the police, but the more weak-willed types (who are usually those chosen by the blackmailer) pay and carry on paying until they can either pay no more or are driven to desperate measures so that payments can be kept up. These measures can take the form of turning to crime, attacking the blackmailer or committing suicide — the latter is the most common.

Summing up at the Old Bailey in 1938, Lord Chief Justice Hewart personalised this conventional association between human waywardness and blackmail:[53]

Let it be granted, that the prosecutor behaved disgracefully, and with treachery to his wife and children. And what about the woman in the dock? It is common ground that she knew he was a married man. Whatever you may think of the prosecutor, what was this on her part but a commercial transaction of the lowest possible kind. You may think that on the facts to talk about sympathy is almost an affront on the English language. You may think, as often happens in disreputable associations of this nature, his appetite began to cool, and he decided to put an end to the association. It may have appeared a somewhat difficult task to him. You know that one of the ingredients in this disreputable association was that they had actually talked of his wife dying, whereupon this woman was to take her place. Anything more disgusting it is difficult to imagine.

Passing sentence, the Lord Chief Justice further observed,

You have been found guilty on the clearest possible evidence of the grave offence of demanding money with menaces. In ordinary circumstances I should pass a sentence of penal servitude, but in your case I shall not take that course. In the point of morals I doubt whether there is anything to choose between you and the prosecutor. The least sentence I can pass upon you is that you be imprisoned for nine months and I recommend you for deportation.

In spite of Lord Chief Justice Hewart's fulmination, the Appeal Court, in a decision to be enshrined in legal history, determined there was some doubt over the clarity of the evidence leading to the conviction of Ilena Bernhard, a divorcee from Hungary. Her sentence was quashed on the grounds that as she honestly believed she was entitled to claim compensation for the lost relationship between herself and the complainant, then it could be allowed in law she had a claim of right and had not committed a criminal offence.[54] An encounter with the victim, 'Mr A', on a Continental train journey had led to what she

43

certainly construed to be an enduring intimate relationship. Unfortunately 'Mr A' did not share this view. He returned to England and domesticity, where Ilena Bernhard, agitated by the unexpectedly unjust turn of events, sought him out and 'threatened to expose him to his wife, and to the public by means of an announcement in a newspaper unless he paid her the sum of £160 forthwith'. During one interview between them, 'the appellant's threats were overheard by a police officer, who had been within hearing as the result of an arrangement with the prosecutor'.[55]

Basil Tozer set out a specification of situations where blackmailers may be found. The moralistic overtones are obvious, but they are worth recording because they reveal the predominant preoccupations of those sufficiently concerned to pronounce publicly on the 'blackmail menace' in the 1920s:

(1)   'Psychoanalysis and Blackmail' — as outlined above.

(2)   'The Good Samaritan's Reward' — a wealthy man typically takes in an ill-looking youth out of sympathy for his condition and is later blackmailed over alleged or actual homosexual exchanges.

(3)   'Obscene Photographs and Blackmail' — victims are usually 'elderly and well-to-do men of no occupation' who secretly buy such photographs and are then threatened with exposure by the salesmen. Such men are prone to blackmail because, although they are outwardly respectable, inside they really have nasty minds.

(4)   'Newspaper Blackmail' — described earlier in this chapter.

(5)   'Dope and Blackmail' — dope peddlers who subsequently blackmail their clients.

(6)   'Photography and Blackmail' — based upon photographs taken whilst the victim was engrossed in what he took or she took to be private and personal leisure activities. Tozer observes in this brief section that for 'an obvious reason it is not possible to publish all that might be told regarding the abominable practices of certain blackmailers'

(7)   'Blackmailers in Bogus Nursing Homes' — male or female nurses have an affair with patients in certain private nursing homes, leading to eventual blackmail.

(8)   'Nosey-Parker Blackmailers'

(9)   'Confiding Domestic Servants' — unexpectedly Tozer here refers to salesmen who persuade maidservants to buy goods on instalments and then frighten them into paying each month.

(10) 'Nude Dancing' — victims are taken to 'fig-leaf performances' and later blackmailed over this discreet interest.[56]

There Tozer's list of predominantly sexual temptations ends. It does, however hint that a more general and important point will bear repetition; the extension of the concept of blackmail from simple extortion to include threats against reputation augmented problems of description and analysis demanding increasing subtlety when clarifying the nature of a threatening demand. For this reason the stereotype of true blackmail developed into a crucially important social yardstick: it deflected attention away from the complex origins of the offence and highlighted the allegedly predictable course it would follow unless checked. There is a fair amount of general agreement on the interdependence of character assassination and moral murder; a comparison between various published materials and reports of blackmail trials shows that the stereotype does incorporate *certain aspects of selected blackmail transactions.*[57] Thus this comparative exercise also reveals that many blackmail transactions only *partially* resemble the stereotype; when it becomes obvious in criminal prosecutions that in many respects detected blackmailers do not reflect their stereotypical counterpart, and the transactions themselves hold many anomalies, the stereotype is transformed conveniently into a notional criterion for the determination of individualised degrees of guilt and innocence. It is at this point that the second aspect of the double-edged stereotype of blackmail, the 'master blackmailer', comes into its own.

Chapter 3

The Master Blackmailer

Next in importance to personal freedom is immunity from suspicious and jealous observation. Men may do without restraints upon their liberty; they may pass to and fro at pleasure; but if their steps are tracked by spies and informers, their associations watched as conspirators — who shall say that they are free?

Sir Erskine May [1]

When Sir Arthur Conan Doyle created perhaps the archetypal fictional master blackmailer, Charles Augustus Milverton, he represented him as a man making a handsome living out of commercial research.[2]

His method is as follows: he allows it to be known that he is prepared to pay very high sums for letters which compromise people of wealth and position. He receives these wares not only from treacherous valets or maids, but frequently from genteel ruffians who have gained the confidence and affection of trusting women. He deals with no niggard hand. I happen to know that he paid seven hundred pounds to a footman for a note two lines in length, and that the ruin of a noble family was the result. Everything which is in the market goes to Milverton, and there are hundreds in this great city who turn white at his name. No one knows where his grip may fall, for he is far too rich and far too cunning to work from hand to mouth. He will hold a card back for years in order to play it at the moment when the stake is best worth winning.

Milverton — 'the worst man in London' — possesses the requisite organisational and commercial skills to conduct large-scale blackmail. But he possesses more than these: the impetus behind his activities is a pathological pattern of motivation, setting him in sharp relief from the rest of humanity and indeed other criminals. He is at all times prepared to profit from the information in his possession; he has no honourable sense of commercial restraint. Unlike the villains in many of the other Sherlock Holmes stories, the presence of Milverton in London threatens not just one or two individual victims but a much larger proportion of respectable society; his existence is portrayed as a danger to a wide number of unspecified people occupying social positions buttressing the legitimate social order. When Sherlock Holmes and Dr Watson are the concealed witnesses of Milverton's murder by one of his well-connected, victims — 'You will ruin no more lives as you ruined mine. You will wring no more hearts as you wrung mine. I will free the world of a poisonous thing' — they keep their knowledge from the police and secretly rejoice that what appeared to be an impregnable menace has been removed for ever.

Within and without the world of fiction the overall stereotype of blackmail defines the master blackmailer as the major source of true blackmail. He is a shadowy, elusive figure, rarely appearing in the criminal courts, but ultimately responsible for pervasive, hidden blackmail. The master blackmailer is symbolised as responsible for the general danger of blackmail in society; he is at heart a strategist and knows how to commercialise cultural norms and to profit from the legitimate social order. Before looking at the collection of unworthy skills said to characterise the master blackmailer, and account for his facility in evading detection, it is worth recalling a massive attempt at pseudo-blackmail by Thomas Neill Cream, druggist's traveller, extensively reported in 'The Times' of 1892.[3]

Case V (pseudo blackmail)   Some months before this case opened at Bow Street police court, two girls, Alice Marsh and Emma Shrivell had been found dying of poison in Stamford Street, London. On 25 April a Dr Harper of Barnstaple received this letter:

London, 25 April, 1892

Dr Harper, Barnstaple.
Dear Sir,
    I am writing to inform you that one of my operators has undisputable evidence that your son, W.J. Harper, a medical student at St Thomas's Hospital, poisoned two girls named Alice Marsh and Emma Shrivell on the 12th inst., and that I am willing to give you the said evidence (so that you can suppress it) for the sum of £1500 sterling. The evidence in my hands is strong enough to convict and hang your son, but I shall give it to you for £1500 sterling, or sell it to the police for the same amount. The publication of the evidence will ruin you and your family for ever, and you know that as well as I do. To show you that what I am writing is true, I am willing to send you a copy of the evidence against your son, so that when you read it you will need no one to tell you that it will convict your son. Answer my letter at once through the columns of the London Daily Chronicle as follows: — 'W.H.M. — will pay you for your services. — Dr H.' After I see this in paper I will communicate with you

47

again. As I said before, I am perfectly willing to satisfy you that I have strong evidence against your son by giving you a copy of it before you pay me a penny.

If you do not answer it at once, I am going to give evidence to the Coroner at once.

Yours respectfully,
W.H. Murray.

Accompanying the letter were several newspaper cuttings dealing with the deaths of the girls, and an elegantly printed circular referring to a third previous death from strychnine:

Ellen Donworth's death. To the guests of the Metropole Hotel.

Ladies and Gentlemen, I hereby notify you that the person who poisoned Ellen Donworth on 13th last October is today in the employ of the Metropole Hotel and that your lives are in danger as long as you remain in this hotel.

Yours respectfully,
W.H. Murray.

London, April 1892.

Prosecuting counsel stated that Ellen Donworth was a girl who had died under mysterious circumstances. Giving evidence, Dr Harper said that on receiving the letter he had shown it to his solicitor and then locked it in a drawer pending the arrival of his son, who came home on 12 May. On 1 June, Dr Harper and his son met Inspector Tonbridge of Scotland Yard and gave him the documents described.

The coroner who presided at the inquest of Alice Marsh and Emma Shrivell said that before opening the enquiry into these deaths he himself received a letter asking him to pass on a second enclosed letter to the foreman of the jury:

London, 2 May.

To the Foreman of the Coroner's Jury, in the Cases
    of Alice Marsh and Emma Shrivell.
Dear Sir,

I beg to inform you that one of my operators has positive proof that Walter Harper, a medical student of St Thomas's Hospital, and a son of Dr Harper, of Bear Street, Barnstaple, is responsible for the deaths of Alice Marsh and of Emma Shrivell, he having poisoned those girls with strychnine. That proof you can have on paying my bill for services to George Clarke, detective, 20 Cockspur Street, Charing Cross, to whom I will give the proof on his paying my bill.

Yours respectfully,
Wm. H. Murray.

A private enquiry agent then attested to receiving a letter on 4 May:

To George Clarke, Esq., Detective,
    20 Cockspur Street, Charing Cross.

London, 4 May, 1892

Dear Sir,
    If Mr Wyatt, Coroner, calls on you in regard to the murders of
Alice Marsh and Emma Shrivell, you can tell him that you will give
proof positive to him that W.H. Harper, student, of St Thomas's
Hospital; and son of Dr Harper, Bear Street, Barnstaple, poisoned
those girls with strychnine, provided the Coroner will pay you well
for your services. Proof of this will be forthcoming. I will write you
again in a few days.

Yours respectfully,
Wm. H. Murray.

Clarke said he never heard from the writer again and did not know him at
all.
    As the case dramatically unfolded it became evident that Cream's
activities had not been confined to 1892. Prosecuting counsel eventually
produced two similar letters to the ones already quoted but posted the
year before. The following was to Dr W.H. Broadbent of Portland
Square:

London, Nov 28, 1891.
Sir, Miss Clover, who until a short time ago lived at 27 Lambeth Road,
S.E., died at the above address on October 20 (last month) through
being poisoned with strychnine. After her death a search of her
affects was made, and evidence was found which showed that you not
only gave her the medicine which caused her death, but that you had
been hired for the purpose of poisoning her. The evidence is in the
hands of one of our detectives, who will give the evidence either to
you or to the police authorities for the sum of £2,500 (two thousand
five hundred pounds sterling). You can have the evidence for £2,500
and in that way save yourself from ruin. If the matter is disposed of
to the police it will be made public by being published in the papers,
and ruin you forever. You know well enough that an accusation of
that sort will ruin you forever. Now, Sir, if you want the evidence
for £2,500, just put a personal in the 'Daily Chronicle' saying you
will pay Malone £2,500 for his services, and I will send a party to
settle this matter. If you do not want the evidence of course, it
will be turned over to the police at once and published, and your
ruin will surely follow. Think well before you decide on this
matter. It is just this — £2,500 sterling on the one hand, and ruin,

shame and disgrace on the other. Answer by personal on the first page of the 'Daily Chronicle' any time next week. I am not humbugging you. I have evidence strong enough to ruin you forever.   M. Malone.

A further letter, posted by Cream in 1891 to the Honourable Frederick Smith of W.H. Smith & Son, was opened by a partner in the firm:

Sir, On Tuesday night, 13th October (last month), a girl named Ellen Donworth, but sometimes calling herself Ellen Linnell, who lived at 8 Duke Street, Westminster Bridge Road, was poisoned with strychnine. After her death, among her effects were found two letters incriminating you, which, if ever they become public property, will surely convict you of the crime. I enclose you a copy of one of the letters, which the girl received on the morning of 13th October (the day on which she died). Just read it, and then judge for yourself what hope you have of escape if the law officers ever get hold of those letters. Think of the shame and disgrace it will bring on your family if you are arrested and put in prison for this crime. My object in writing you is to ask if you will retain me at once as your counsellor and legal adviser. If you employ me at once to act for you in this matter, I will save you from all exposure and shame in the matter; but if you will wait till arrested before retaining me, then I cannot act for you, as no lawyer can save you after the authorities get hold of those two letters. If you wish to retain me, just write a few lines on paper, saying, 'Mr Fred Smith wishes to see Mr Bayne, the barrister, at once'. Paste this on one of your shop windows at 186 Strand next Tuesday morning, and when I see it I will drop in and have a private interview with you. I can save you if you retain me in time, but not otherwise.
Yours truly,
Mr Frederick Smith   H. Bayne.

The enclosure referred to in the letter ran as follows:

Miss Ellen Linnel, I wrote and warned you once before that Frederick Smith of W.H. Smith & Son was going to poison you, and I am writing now to say that if you take any of the medicine he gave you you will die. I saw Frederick Smith prepare the medicine he gave you and I saw him put enough strychnine in the medicine to kill a horse. If you take any of it you will die.
H.M.B.

This was handed to a solicitor of the firm and afterwards to the police. A handwriting expert stated that the prisoner was undoubtedly the sole author of all the letters.

Almost inevitably, Cream's tortuous plot to enmesh others — to redirect suspicion of murder — failed. He succeeded only in enmeshing himself. Once evidence that he was the author of the blackmail letters began to accumulate Cream was remanded at Bow Street Police Court, and later successfully prosecuted for the murder of Matilda Clover, the other three deaths providing corroborative evidence.[4]

Extensive coverage of the case in 'The Times', gives some indication of the interest it aroused,[5] and I have quoted Cream's letters in full because they give some insight into the social mechanisms he thought he could bring into play in his favour. Undoubtedly he adopted the form of the master blackmailer — unfortunately he lacked the substance.

W. Teignmouth Shore, in his discussion of Cream's trial for murder, observes that Cream had successfully practised the interconnected trades of abortionist and blackmailer in the past but in this instance he could hardly be seriously accused of attempting blackmail. 'In this case . . . Cream seems not to have made any effort to follow up his threats, and cannot, as was surmised, have made his living as a blackmailer'.[6] The whole affair had passed out of his control: he was desperately reduced to emulating the tactics of the master blackmailer to cover his own unpleasant crimes.

The stereotype of the master blackmailer is not one which lays emphasis on visible external characteristics. It is characterological, summarising a series of defined and well-concealed skills, coupled with pathological personality traits motivating the blackmailer to initiate the transaction, and to carry out his threats to reveal discrediting information if crossed.

C.J. Ettinger, a psychiatrist and Professor of Sociology, writing in America in the early 1930s, summed up the stereotype of the master blackmailer as the author of true blackmail:[7]

The blackmailers play their cards with the greatest boldness, knowing well there is little danger of exposure or prosecution. And when the victim has paid, as he thinks, the price of his escape from publicity, he awakes to learn that the blackmailers have him securely in their clutches and that for the remainder of his life he must pay a regular weekly or monthly stipend as the price of his security from scandal. The blackmailer never relents — once a victim, always a victim. One such unfortunate provides a life income for the blackmailer. Thus it is that many of the blackmail rings have regular payments from victims, very much as a retired capitalist has a regular income from the rent from his different business properties or dividends from his stocks and bonds.

One of those extreme instances of detected blackmail, lending some credibility to the concept of the master blackmailer was the well-documented 'Mr A Case'. It all started as a civil action by Charles Ernest Robinson, a bookmaker, to recover £125,000 from the Midland Bank — money which he said had been paid into an account for his use and had been negligently paid out by the bank to someone else.

As the hearing progressed it became obvious that the money involved was a share of a much larger sum, obtained through a blackmail conspiracy hovering around 'Mr A', an Indian Prince. 'Mr A' had an affair with Mrs Robinson which others, whether they had contrived it or not, had certainly turned to their advantage. A jury later found that Robinson and his wife, whose adultery with the Prince gave the blackmailers the leverage they required, were not parties to the original conspiracy. At the same time, the original civil case and later proceedings revealed that a man who had played an apparently major role in this 'high society' version of the 'badger game',[8] was William Cooper Hobbs.

Writing his foreword to the printed transcript of Robinson's original unsuccessful civil action, C.E. Bechhofer Roberts described the case, taking place towards the end of 1924, as eclipsing,[9]

all previously revealed examples of its kind (and, one may justifiably assume, all unrevealed ones as well) by the magnitude of the sum involved; the victim parted with cheques for no less than £300,000 as hush-money to the scoundrels who beset him, though it is true, half this sum never reached their pockets.

Bechhofer Roberts also describes William Cooper Hobbs (who acted as a go-between for the parties to the transaction, and who was later prosecuted at the Old Bailey for criminal conspiracy), as

The black sheep of a respectable family — his father had been a freeman of the City of London — Hobbs had discovered early in life a flair for the seamier side of the law. From the turn of the century he persuaded one obscure solicitor after another to set up an office with himself as the real principal. There were and still are, many opportunities in London for an unscrupulous law firm — claims arising out of the fantastic English law of libel are only one of the profitable openings — and Hobbs fully exploited the position. He had a wide knowledge of the bye-ways of English procedure, so galling and expensive to litigants; he knew exactly how to put pressure on unwilling opponents and willing witnesses, and he had valuable contacts with the more enterprising criminal classes. He also conducted a money-lending business which he found both profitable in itself and convenient as a mask for more scandalous enterprises.

By the time the 'Mr A Case' had reached public attention, Hobbs was a sick and ageing man. But he had acquired a persistent deviant identity, which reflected in its various facets certain crucial attributes of the fictional master blackmailer. Sergeant Sullivan, who was briefed by Hobbs in two libel actions against newspapers he believed had over-dramatised his criminality, could scarcely conceal his distaste. Sullivan was troubled throughout their association because professional ethics required him to play the role of devil's advocate on behalf of a man against whom the Lord Chief Justice showed considerable hostility: 'Indeed he made it perfectly obvious that he considered it was an insult to himself that I should appear before him and address the jury on behalf of Hobbs'. 'No one', added Sullivan, 'hated Hobbs more than I did'.[10]

If we move on from this rather unusual case to take an overview of criminal blackmail, we can list the outstanding characteristics of the master blackmailer as follows:

(1)   camouflage: the master blackmailer is not detectable, he merges into the surroundings;

(2)   subtlety: one of his most effective methods of avoiding detection is to work as far as possible within the law, and to present his demands with grace;

(3)   calculating rationality: there is no sentiment in business;

(4)   worldliness: the master blackmailer is a 'man of the world' who knows how to resist temptation;

(5)   special expertise in the accumulation of commercial information: he represents the focal point of an expanding network of communications;

(6)   professional discretion: he keeps his word so long as the bargain is in operation;

(7)   multiple clientele: the master blackmailer is a mass blackmailer.

All these qualities are responsive to an evil and merciless love of money and power. Above all, the master blackmailer is in control both of himself and the situation.

For blackmail on this scale to remain successful, and undetected, certain refinements become essential, and the stereotype carries overt connotations of social class. The master blackmailer is rarely portrayed as a member of the vulgar criminal underworld, enmeshed in the vice trade; rather he is a pseudo-respectable figure, several stages removed from any demonstrable connection with criminality, and protected by an impregnable façade. Courtroom proceedings yield little evidence to confirm the existence of such remarkable practitioners; those blackmailers who come to light do so because their identities are known to the victim, the master would never wind up in the sort of situation neatly summarised in a court report of 1896:[11]

> When she met the prisoner on Wednesday afternoon she asked him what he wanted. He said that if she would give him anything, however small, he did not mind. She asked him how much he wanted, but he refused to name any sum saying, 'Because you might give me in charge of blackmailing'. She asked him three or four times to name the sum, and he always gave the same reply. She said, 'What will you do if I do not give you any money? '. He replied, 'I shall make the affair public'. She then gave him in charge, a police officer being near at the time.

The master blackmailer knows how not to appear to be making a demand; he is skilled in the regretful presentation of the implied threat:[12]

> The popular conception of a blackmailer is a man of little education and less character whose appearance and manner suggest something better than a burglar and something less than a defaulting cashier. As a matter of fact, the uneducated — I use the word in its conventional dictionary meaning — blackmailer has an exceedingly short life and a far from merry one. He risks a heavy sentence of penal servitude for the sake of a few hundred pounds and he relies on mere chance for opportunity for practising his special form of crime.

We need not look simply at accounts by those whose lives have brought them into some sort of contact with 'the criminal classes' to read about the oft-affirmed characteristics of the master blackmailer. Charles Augustus Howell, friend, acquaintance, and business agent, of some of the prominent creative artists of the latter half of the nineteenth century, including Rossetti and Ruskin, managed to acquire an unenviable reputation as a possible blackmailer without ever going near the criminal courts. So effectively that H. Rossetti Angeli published a biography of Howell in an attempt to rescue his memory, and to distinguish him, as a businessman who had acquired rather a shady reputation, from the stereotypical blackmailer.[13]

> The blackest interpretation [she wrote] has been placed on his every action and he alone blamed for every breach or cessation of friendship.

It is quite unfair to suspect him of a propensity to blackmail, though the ugly word has more than once been coupled with his name. Sharer, as he was of many indiscreet confidences and recipient of many a letter that it would have been more prudent not to have written, there is no evidence that he ever sought to levy vile profit from these. His worst offence is that he did not destroy the letters and that he was suspected of talking flippantly of some of the confidences.

As William Rossetti, brother of the poet and painter Dante Gabriel, wrote of Howell, in an edition of Dante Gabriel's letters:[14]

As a salesman — with his open manner, his winning address, and his exhaustless gift of amusing talk, not innocent of high colouring and of actual blague — Howell was unsurpassable; and he achieved for Rossetti, with ease and also with much ingenious planning, many a stroke of most excellent professional business, such as other men, less capable of playing upon the hobbies and weaknesses of their fellow-creatures, would have found arduous or impossible.

The blackmailer in the courts

By and large convicted blackmailers form part of that army of known offenders who have proved an ornament and a justification to British criminology for some years: the incompetent, the disorganised, and those who are simply unlucky. They are the ones who fall into the hands of the police, either because they are unable to resist the immediately pressing nature of their financial needs, or because they hurriedly miscalculate, thus overcoming the victim's reluctance to go to the authorities. Detected blackmailers can, of course, initiate true blackmail; for instance, in 1933, the police described a woman who received three years penal servitude for sending demanding letters to a company director (Mr K), as 'an unscrupulous, dangerous, and heartless woman, essentially a blackmailer and a vulgar thief'.[15] Professional blackmailers do not of course present themselves publicly as either dangerous or heartless: wandering through London's 'underworld' in the second decade of this century, Mrs Cecil Chesterton encountered a group of old women who 'might have been a sewing-party in a parish room'. They were scouring the Sunday papers for possible blackmail victims. Patient research could, she alleged, provide a 'small but steady investment' for ladies clinging tightly to their outward respectability: ex-professional women of an uncertain age, running crime on a business footing, and living quiet domestic lives.[16]

The authorities are fully aware that offenders appearing before the courts scarcely resemble the full stereotype. Fining a youth £50 for having obtained £234 from another by threatening to inform his father he had bought a motor scooter against his wishes, the chairman of a juvenile court told the youngster his action was 'despicable': 'It is one of the worst offences we can imagine, but we are allowing you to go home because of the excellent reports we have had about you'. On behalf of a woman who pleaded guilty at Winchester Assizes to sending letters demanding £250 from a man in Bath (alleging he was the father of her child), it was said her husband had a good position and she did not need any money. She had been distressed over the death of her child and the letters were written six weeks prior to the birth of another; her weakened state of health had made her the easy victim of fortune tellers.[17]

A few years before, at the same Assizes, a Portsmouth electrician was charged with demanding £50 from a women to whose daughter he was supposed to be engaged. The letter he sent to her contained the words: 'I have happened upon a certain well-known person, and have concluded that it is to your advantage to keep dark certain facts which concern that person.' Police evidence characterised the writer as 'a mean and despicable fraud endeavouring to maintain a social position entirely beyond his means'. He received eighteen months imprisonment with hard labour. Significantly, the judge said that but for his youth, and the fact that the blackmailing letter was so clumsy, he would have awarded the defendant penal servitude.[18]

It is is immaterial whether a court actually perceives a given defendant as possessing *all* the requisite attributes of the 'master blackmailer'; what is important is that the court's reported reaction to the offence confirms the argument that the true cause of evil blackmail is the presence in the world of 'unprincipled, scheming and devious' people who are peculiarly vicious. Offenders who are not labelled master blackmailers by the courts are often on the receiving end of this dispensation because they can convince the courts that their behaviour was inspired not by abiding criminal motives, but was the result of a thoughtless response to unique situational pressures.

Diagnosed mental illness, often unspecified, can effectively rob an accusation of blackmail of its sting. Just after the last war a woman attempting to blackmail an elderly and respectable man, who had responded to an advert she had placed in the local paper offering massage and psychological help, was examined by a prison doctor. The ensuing opinion was that, although not certifiable, the defendant was suffering from a marked degree of 'mental instability bordering on insanity'. As a result of this report she was bound over for two years — a lenient sentence for blackmail — on condition that she went to mental hospital as a voluntary patient. On the other hand penal servitude for three years was prescribed for a valet after he sent the letters quoted below to the wife of Arthur Greenwood, the Minister of Health in 1931. The police stated that the author of the letters had previously been arrested in London for disorderly conduct; seemingly he had wanted to see the Lord Mayor to get him to give a letter on his behalf to the King, which he hoped would help him find his relatives. He was later remanded to a mental home and some time after released as cured.

The first letter:

Mrs Arthur Greenwood, wife of the Minister of Health. This is an emphatic warning that failure on your part to remit without delay £500 16s 1½d will cause me to carry out my intention of greeting both of you with a bottle of vitriol.

You are asking to have your haunt burgled. Rest assured no time will be lost in that respect. Such as you are the cause of the chaos prevailing in England.

was followed by:

Greenwood, Madhouse Keeper, £500 is the sum I demand from you for your trickery on February 5th last. You in your exalted position ought to set a noble example, you scoundrel. Bear in mind members of your family will sustain trouble unless or until I get redress you will receive what you need most — vitriol. Your haunts are all get-at-able.

The judge told the prisoner he thought he was mad and if he was he would be sent to Broadmoor for the rest of his life, or until he was cured. 'The lives of public men are not going to be rendered more difficult than they are by nuisances like you'.[19]

For the purposes of conventional criminal justice, the stereotype of the master blackmailer is imported to help judge the seriousness of the offence and to apportion blame. An integral feature of any prosecution is a comparison of alleged accounts of the offence with the stereotype of blackmail, to determine the extent to which the actions and motives of the accused can be seen to correspond with those of the 'master blackmailer'.

Recognition by the courts, and the penal system, of degrees of criminality leads to recognition of degrees of evil possession of the defendant by the mischievous impulse to blackmail.[20] This does not mean the alleged offender will necessarily be acquitted but it may enable him to claim that his actions were not those of a true blackmailer,

especially if (as is often the case) he has no previous criminal record.
Here is an example of a bid for favourable interpretation of an alleged
blackmailing offence:[21]

> My act was one of madness, in a fit of desperation, due to debts
> and my inability to obtain capital for my invention. Further my
> home was in jeopardy. I do not know 'Dr X', neither do I know
> anything against him whatsoever, and in all sincerity I seek his
> pardon and offer him my most humble apology for the great wrong
> I have done him. I deeply regret my action, which has brought
> nothing but sorrow, pain, and extreme embarrassment to my people,
> and I fully realise the seriousness of it now. I plead, therefore, for
> the mercy of this court, 'Dr X' in a manner apart from pleading
> the First Offender's Act. Further, I give my word never to offend
> either the law or my people ever again . . . I am pleading guilty, but
> without malicious intent.

Following a single offence in an otherwise unremarkable life, a
person may be classified a criminal blackmailer, and publicly disclaim
the validity of the label:[22]

> I should like to say that I am not the vile blackmailer that I have
> been called in this court. As an ex-British Blue jacket four months
> ago I had an honour which was a thing unassailable. We know we
> have done wrong and we know we expect to be punished for it,
> but I should like to say we have been eleven weeks in prison and in
> those eleven weeks we have suffered miseries beyond belief. I say
> we touched the utmost depths of human misery in those weeks, and
> we have lost everything there is in the world worth living for except
> our love for one another, and I am going to ask you, My Lord, to
> look on what we have done as something foolish rather than
> criminal. ι know I have said things I had no right to say, but I do
> say I considered that this money we were entitled to. I admit I
> did go the wrong way about it, and if I cause Mrs — a lot of
> unpleasantness I am very sorry. The whole of the case arose from
> nothing more or less than a drunken brawl.

Offenders before the courts, are often warned by the judge they
have *unsuccessfully played the role of the blackmailer*. Two men
received seven years imprisonment for plotting to blackmail a doctor,
some of his women patients, and their relatives, through threats to
reveal details of abortions contained in medical records they had
stolen. Passing sentence the judge informed them: 'I accept that
there were others involved who were perhaps the prime movers but

you certainly played your parts'.

Inevitably the detected blackmailer, rather like the amateur respectable shoplifter described by Mary Owen Cameron,[23] starts off with a disadvantage. Unlike the professional, he or she is ill-prepared to negotiate the complex ramifications of the law.[24] As we have seen such blackmailers are often caught in the act: they write letters either in traceable handwriting and notepaper, or conveniently signed, they reveal themselves apparently indiscriminately to victims and their companions, and they often plead guilty at least to the technical illegality of blackmail. Furthermore, unlike the respectable shoplifter, who may more readily be excused responsibility for his or her actions, the detected blackmailer has done something very terrible and has aroused considerable anxiety.

Since it is plain to all involved that many prosecuted offenders are not engaged in the rational deployment of high grade skills, the most helpful category of the stereotype of the master blackmailer is 'moral unworthiness'.[25] Moral unworthiness is the key to the parasitology of blackmail. More often than not it is this 'personality model' which is used by the court to explain blackmail, on the grounds that the penal system cannot dispose of the accused in any other way. The decisive factor here is the demonstrable preoccupation of the offender with personal gain: greed is the one personality trait linking the detected 'real life' blackmailer with the stereotypical master. Greed, coupled of course with an inordinate lust for power, is the driving force behind true blackmail.

Although the stereotype cannot fully explain detected blackmail, it can be used to justify the punishment of individual rule-breakers, and it fulfils three other social requirements:

(1)   It collectively categorises the mixed bag of individuals who sporadically become known to the police. Grouping together detected blackmailers has the additional pay-off of providing an administratively viable explanation of why they are there. By extension, concealed offences may be attributed to a master figure who can evade detection.

(2)   It helps locate the presence of criminals and near-criminals, prone to initiate blackmail, whose company all right-thinking people should avoid.

(3)   By providing an 'identikit' picture of unworthy criminality, the stereotype (in both its complementary manifestations, true blackmail and the master-blackmailer), stands as a yardstick against which degrees of criminal intentionality can be attributed to those who are prosecuted. This assists the relative exoneration of the victim and the maintenance of his image of respectability, What Troy Duster has called 'total' stigmatisation[26] may envelope the blackmailer in court, whereas, ii at all, the victim is only likely to be partially stigmatised.

Thus the stereotyping process helps to dramatise what has been called 'an imaginary social order'.[27] In court we are offered types of ideals rather than ideal types. The place of the accused throughout criminal proceedings symbolises a threat to conventional values: he cannot be trusted to keep secrets. Stereotyping the offender helps ironically to stereotype normality. Whilst the meaning of blackmail is familiar to us — we 'know' what the word means — criminal prosecutions help to make the familiar, unfamiliar, or strange and outrageous.

If, at this stage, we dare risk any judgment about the role of the stereotype, it is that the trial brings about not so much an affirmation of collective solidarity, but rather an indication of hierarchical social differentiation. By turning a blind eye to the possibly deviant activity of the victim the blackmail trial upholds the ideology of respectability.

Since of necessity the reputational blackmailer makes us all the potential accomplices of his crime we must, when news reaches us, put up some resistance, we do not see ourselves as criminals or destructive of the lives of others. To stigmatise the victim in court would affirm explicitly our involvement in the blackmailer's crime; the stereotype of blackmail facilities a denial of complicity and this is why it is purely retributive.

Chapter 4

The Business
of Blackmail

Respectability . . . wasn't it safe, after all? How glibly could one
maintain . . . that it guaranteed every man a living?

George Dangerfield[1]

Notwithstanding the retributive stigmatisation inherent in the stereotype,
reputational blackmail can hardly be totally separated from the wider
socio-economic matrix of human relations. A now forgotten writer,
A.R.L. Gardner, included, in a study of various kinds of law-breaking,
published in 1931, a short chapter describing six contemporary cases of
blackmail.[2] What is remarkable about this chapter — 'Suppliers of
Illicit Desires, And Blackmailers' — is the ironic treatment Gardner gives
his subject matter; specifically via his comments on the interdependence
of social acceptability and respectable reputation. Having pointed out
that it is the task of professional blackmailers to prey on the hidden
illegalities and weaknesses of various members of the community
(including any behaviour 'derogatory to his reputation in the eyes of
those whose approval he values'), Gardner concludes his chapter with
the words, 'most people are afraid not of being what they seem to be,
but of seeming to be what they are in a land so pledged to respectability'.
He finds the familiar unwillingness of victims to seek the protection of
the authorities unsurprising, 'if by so doing they find themselves obliged
to confess, or at any rate suggest, that their behaviour falls short of that
level of conventionality to which it is the wish of most people to appear
to conform'.

Just as in court witnesses have to provide 'evidence of respectability'
from time to time, so in other spheres of life individuals are required to
proffer some evidence of their essential respectability if they wish to
succeed in the legitimate world. Recently it has been claimed that we
all live in a 'credential society' where 'credentialism assures *personal*
acceptability', and those possessing the necessary paper qualifications
'have demonstrated that they can get by, get along with others, conform,

61

manage'.[3] Nowadays respectability is invested with a much wider significance than the traditional meaning of monogamous sexuality, but it is still firmly linked with the maintenance of an honourable public reputation as a means of achieving outward social acceptability in a competitive hierarchical society. To put it another way, respectability is best summarised in the popular obituary: 'there never was a word said against him'.

Sociologist Donald Ball has defined the phenomenon as a 'central concern of actors in the problematic dramas of mundane life'. Furthermore,[4]

> it seems that historically this has particularly been the case since the nineteenth century . . . and although the quest for respectability is perhaps not as frenzied as it was in the Victorian era — for instance, when censors were concerned to bowdlerise Shakespeare and even Robinson Crusoe and the entire socio-cultural milieu was organised around respectability-centred norms and values — it is still a major focus in day-to-day practical affairs.

In the sense Ball uses the term, respectability is crucially bound up with two sets of interrelated social factors:

(1)   actors and audiences: those whose perceived behaviour is exposed to the judgment of others and the actual personnel making an evaluation at the time;

(2)   ideologies of moral worth coupled with 'the belief in the accuracy or "rightness" of these judgments'.[5]

The experience of blackmail is one response to these two sets of social pressures:

> If your social and business people knew you they would drop you like a hot brick.

> I have given a great deal of thought to this matter and gone into detail of possible gain or loss.

> If I lose you lose. And you have more to lose than I have. If I win, you win, apart from losing a little money.

> Please do not underestimate my determination. I am a Virgo, as you are and once having embarked on something we Virgos don't turn back and in this case I hold all the aces.

To be of good report is to retain a foothold in the world — to 'make a living'. The loss of respectable reputation, or the emergence of an uncreditable social image which mars easy and progressive interaction with others, can have far-reaching consequences for one's practical life chances and consequent self-esteem.[6] The possession of a respectable reputation in turn confirms one's position in a prized social milieu.

A stage actor, accused of conspiring with a colleague to blackmail an unnamed candidate in the General Election of 1929 described a conversation with the victim. He was posing as a private detective and had called on the candidate:[7]

I saw him [i.e. the candidate] and said, 'I am making enquiries about a woman named Smith. I understand you are acquainted with her!' (Allegedly this woman had an illegitimate child after being seduced by the candidate.) Then I read him a sort of lecture. I said it was very foolish of him, considering he was entering into public life, carrying on an intrigue like that. If it came into the hands of unscrupulous people it might do him an injury. He agreed that it might. He asked if the enquiry came from a member of a certain club whom he had refused a loan of £400. I said, 'Oh, no, it is a political stunt! He asked me what I was going to do about it. I said, 'If I don't send in the report as true there will be an end of it!' He said, 'If you do that it will be worth a good deal to me!' I said, 'It may be worth a tip!' We arranged to meet next day at Waterloo Station.

Of course, the financial, legal, and other social penalties of exposure of information about the life of a potential victim vary. Not all individuals show themselves willing to treat with would-be blackmailers:

Case VI (attempted blackmail)   Colchester police court in 1894 witnessed charges brought against a middle-aged unmarried woman with attempting to obtain £300 menaces from a doctor. The doctor on the receiving end of these demands had been the family physician for many years. By the time the case had progressed to Chelmsford Assizes, in the next year, the defendant had pleaded guilty to sending a telegram and a letter to the doctor demanding financial help.

During the original court proceedings it transpired the accused had first called at the doctor's surgery 'in a most excited condition', saying she had quarrelled with her parents and was determined to go to London. She asked for money for the journey. This was apparently given, the donor prudently informing the parents of what had taken place; once in London the defendant wrote again asking for more money which again the doctor provided, this time informing his own wife and relatives. Shortly after he treated the woman for an internal ailment 'through the post'.

On 20 September 1894, the doctor was summoned to the Lion

Hotel in Colchester to find his patient in an excited state. She had, he said, become involved financially with a Mrs Macbeath of London to whom she now owed £180, and could she have the money. At first he refused but finally agreed to make a loan at 5 per cent, receiving an IOU note in return. He then informed the defendant's parents of this transaction. Some days later, both doctor and father went to London to be greeted with the explanation that she had needed the £180 to take a lodging house as a secret place where she and the doctor could meet. Eventually she threatened to expose the doctor's sexual gyrations unless he paid her £300; in the police court she produced a long written statement accusing the doctor of having seduced her in his surgery, and of regular intimacy ever since.

One of the most interesting things about this case is the reported reaction of the doctor to the allegations brought against him. Counsel for the prosecution said at Chelmsford Assizes he 'was so well known in Colchester that it was not suggested that the unfounded accusations made against him by the prisoner had in any way injured his reputation'. Seemingly, some men are so secure in their reputations that blackmail threats do not unsettle them. Temporarily at least, they are in control of their particular life situations and future life chances and like the Duke of Wellington they may advise potential blackmailers to 'publish and be damned'.

In Colchester and London the victim was sustained by the fact that he had attended his accuser 'some years ago for a painful malady peculiar to her sex'. Last June she was in a hysterical condition and left her home to start a boarding house in London. No doubt, stated the prosecution, the accused sent the telegram complained of when in a very weak state of health. The judge allowed her, under her father's recognisances, to come up for judgment if called upon, and on the understanding that she should be looked after at home in order to protect both herself and the doctor from further trouble.[8]

For Victorians the law of libel underscored the commercial value of respectable reputation: 'it attached price tags to everything'. A man's reputation was . . . the tenderest, most vulnerable part of his anatomy, to be legally protected from even the most unintentional attack. Reputations were more jealously guarded in that many of them were no doubt undeserved'.[9] Although there was 'no wholly satisfactory definition of a defamatory imputation',[10] it was possible for those with money to extract large sums in damages from a defendant at a libel prosecution. Willingness to take such action in the pursuit of compensatory or punitive damages depended upon the degree of investment the plaintiff or prosecutor in his or her reputation.[11]

Whilst the criteria of moral worth informing concepts of respectable reputation have changed to some extent since Victoria's reign, the functions of reputation as both a construct and a commodity have not. Louis Blom-Cooper has stressed recently that at the close of a civil action for libel no vindicated plaintiff has so far refused the awarded damages.[12] The fact that this is too much to ask serves to emphasise that reputation has 'gone commercial' if it was not so before. At the time of writing, Mr Justice Faulk's departmental committee on defamation has received a memorandum from the law reform committee of the Law Society. Of the utmost importance, states the memorandum, is that judges and not juries should fix the damages to be paid in libel and slander actions; the process of evaluating an individual's worth depends upon a gamut of elusive considerations to which juries often prove insensitive. Consequently the judge's knowledge of amounts previously awarded in comparable cases is the only guide to the institution and maintenance of more consistent and fairer awards in the future.[13]

Oscar Wilde who rejected proposals from would-be blackmailers summarised the position with customary aplomb when he made one of his characters, the blackmailing Mrs Cheveley, inform her supposed victim she was only attempting to initiate a commercial transaction. 'There is no good mixing up sentimentality in it. I offered to sell Robert Chiltern a certain thing. If he won't pay my price, he will have to pay the world a greater price. There is no more to be said'.[14]

During the course of interaction with others, business and pleasure interpenetrate and it is sometimes not only hard to know where to draw the line but also how to tell one from the other.

Analysing the ways in which the individual human personality is realised through social interaction, Richard Carson has recently written,[15]

> The commodities persons exchange in their relations with each other are many and varied. Such exchanges are typically governed by 'agreements', often tacit and implicit, which state more or less precisely the commodities to be traded and the 'terms' of the trade . . . Generally speaking, mutual acceptance of such an agreement signifies that each party believes that the proposed exchange is at least equal in advantage to those he could effect with others capable of delivering the same desired commodity.

Given the widespread belief in the ubiquity of 'hidden' blackmail, it is reasonable to suppose that many completed transactions do not come to light because they involve exchanges to some extent mutually satisfactory. When an offence *comes to light* it may be:

(1)   the proposed transaction is not acceptable, or is totally

repugnant to the potential victim;

(2)   following a change of heart, or reduced resources, the victim no longer feels able to comply with the blackmailer's demands;

(3)   the person attempting to initiate the transaction is inadequate to the task.

To be successful, reputational blackmail requires a great deal of subtlety and calculation. Drawing together the perspectives of the blackmailer (the perceived source of his sense of power) and the victim (his willingness to reciprocate, at least for a time), is appreciation of reputation as a resource in our society. The reputation of *the victim* represents a livelihood for both parties to the transaction. Simultaneously the present and projected future reputations of *blackmailer and victim* condition and constrain their bargaining power in a variety of ways. Quite obviously neither is operating in a social vacuum; they are acutely conscious of the symbolic presence of a larger audience whose likely reactions they must mentally rehearse to lend credibility and predictability to their calculations:

> I think some people will be very interested to hear what you are up to with your friend. Unless you pay £150 by tomorrow, I shall give your wife the whole story. Give your friend the money. She will know where to take it. Do not think I am joking. I have already told your friend's husband some things about you, so pay up.

Relatively speaking the blackmailer will represent himself as someone who has little to lose — partly because he feels his own reputation is secure. He may not have low status (though more blackmailers in this study worked in occupations at a lower end of the socio-economic scale than their victims), but he is likely to see himself in a position of 'high information control'.[16] Control over the transaction may be enhanced by a hopeful anticipation of the consequences of discovery: short of prosecution and conviction, the blackmailer may expect to find himself cast in the ambiguous role of informer, someone who is not infrequently described as functionally necessary for the maintenance of legitimate social order.[17] However, an even more important safety outlet from the blackmailer's point of view, is the affinity between his role and that of the scandal-monger.[18] Like the informer, the scandal-monger invites others to do his dirty work for him; he can put a considerable distance between himself and his dubious trade. By threatening to transmit discreditable information he does not *necessarily* proclaim any deep-seated commitment to the standards the victim has allegedly violated, he merely proposes to set the judgmental process in motion.

If the blackmailer is to profit he must symbolically mobilise the support of legitimate members of society; his threat must be morally sustained by an invisible accusing army. On 4 February 1930, a labourer at work on a ladder caught sight of a clergyman in a 'compromising situation' in an adjoining building and 'immediately seized upon it to turn it to commercial purposes'. He propositioned the prosecutor, and the following exchange was reported as having taken place between the two men:

Labourer:	'What are you going to do to hush it up?'
Clergyman:	'This is blackmail'.
Labourer:	'That is true. In most cases blackmail continues, but in this case £5 will settle it'.

The labourer then received £2 on account of the £5 promised. In spite of the blackmailer's assurances to the contrary, payments were said to have carried on throughout that year until £100 had been handed over by the victim, described as a man of small means. Later the defendant began making his requests in writing; in one letter he said that if the money was not paid he would see another clergyman, and failing him the bishop, and then they would know what sort of villain the victim had been. The prosecutor then went to the police.[19]

If discreditable information is to raise a scandalised reaction it must be made available at the right moment: what is scandalous at one point in time may be dismissed as irrelevant or pitied as tragic at another. It may lose its force in the 'status politics' of life. In 1936 the 'moral panic' many assumed would follow if news about King Edward VIII's friendship with Mrs Simpson was broadcast to the nation, revealed itself in a letter to the King from his Private Secretary in November: 'The silence of the British Press on the subject of your Majesty's friendship with Mrs Simpson is *not* going to be maintained. It is probably only a matter of days before the outburst begins. Judging by the letters from British subjects living in foreign countries where the Press has been-outspoken, the effect will be calamitous'.[20] The actual scandalised reaction to the possibility of King Edward VIII's marrying Mrs Simpson is now well known:[21]

The marriage of the Sovereign to a woman who had two divorced husbands living raises an extremely different question. Beyond doubt it would cause a deep offence to immense numbers, including a great many who would raise no objection if it were a private individual. A public challenge would be thrown to religious susceptibilities, which, however obsolete they may be considered in this modern world, still have a strong hold on a great multitude. Many others would feel a sense of indignity offered to the great tradition of the Crown.

Nevertheless when the ex-king died in 1972, expressions of regret over the past were voiced in many quarters. 'When tragedy happens in our history', stated the Archbishop of Canterbury in the House of Lords, 'it is natural for us to dwell upon it and try to assess it'.[22]

Amidst fluctuations in the moral temper, the blackmailer must accurately gauge the spirit of his time. His knowledge that the information he possesses is discreditable must be grounded on a realistic appreciation of the direction public disapproval will take, once the word has been passed around. The notion of scandal is inappropriate without complementary cultural models of rectitude and its rewards, constituting an overall symbolic point of reference for conflict and competition over 'the distribution of status and prestige'.[23]

Vulnerability to blackmail

Outwardly perceived patterns of association are thus crucial to the maintenance of a respectable reputation. Those who wish to be of good report must be careful of the audience witnessing their activities.

Case VII (compensatory blackmail)   In May 1885, at Reading Assizes, the keeper of a small temperance hotel in Bristol was indicted on the charge 'of unlawfully threatening to publish matters touching' a clergyman. She had, on her own admission, written two letters to the prosecutor suggesting that he had spent the night at her hotel under an assumed name with a woman formerly his housemaid, who now lodged at the hotel. The letters also alleged that he had two children by this woman and further stated that if the recipient did not come to terms the sender would expose him, if necessary, in his own pulpit.

For the defence it was urged the sole question was whether the letters were written to extort money. These communications it was represented had no greater significance than that the prisoner was considering taking civil proceedings for compensation in a just claim for the injury done to the reputation of her house. On her own behalf the defendant made a long statement justifying her accusations, adding that money was owed by the woman lodging with her and she had been told by the prosecutor she would be paid all that was due to her. At the time of writing the letters, twenty-seven shillings remained outstanding.

Of particular interest to us here is the fact that the prosecuting vicar was subjected by defence counsel to what 'The Times' described as 'a searching cross-examination' where he revealed the bishop of his diocese had required him publicly to clear his character and that he had, prior to these proceedings, taken out a summons for libel against the defendant. He swore that the charges brought against him were false but admitted that fourteen years ago he had seduced the woman concerned and had occasionally encountered her over the succeeding years. Responding to counsel for the prosecution, the vicar added the exonerating claim that he had offered to educate and marry the woman concerned but she would not consent.[24]

Events, actions, and responses constituting the anvil of the individual reputation are situationally and historically specific. The forms and content of public scandal are responsive to stresses and strains in the overall society: scandalous gossip in the later decades of the eighteenth century — the 'Age of Scandal' —[25] was the privileged product of an aristocracy relatively unthreatened from without, and endowed with a sense of social security within.[26]

> The gossip lived in a small society which scarcely touched the middle classes of Wesley, nor the peasantry, nor the Mob . . . They moved in the light world of the Drawing-rooms and of the Birthdays, knew each other as well as the boys at a public school in England might know each other today, chatted about the latest scandal, and, because they had learned to be literate, they wrote it down.

In this enclosed and protected world reputational gossip emerged predominantly as a form of entertainment; the specific judgmental factor, so valuable to the blackmailer, scarcely made its presence felt.

However, times have changed, and the problematic issue of the credibility of the threat of blackmail now arises. Sometimes, to the outside observer, the blackmailer's position appears very weak indeed; it may well seem 'irrational', and hardly calculated to produce the desired effect. A 'gentleman who lived at Eastbourne' received a letter on 9 April 1931, containing this passage:[27]

> I am very anxious to go abroad, but I require the necessary sum to make this possible. I want exactly £500. You will meet my agent tomorrow, April 10, at the lounge at the Strand Palace Hotel and wear two red carnations in your buttonhole. This sounds rather cheaply criminal, but it really is essential, and you will hand my agent a packet containing the sum of £250 in notes of £5. I will not be present and without the money is handed to me within half

an hour after the time mentioned I will immediately make it my business to notify several folk in Eastbourne of the circumstances and as far as I can see your name will be drawn through the mud. This I know is against the law, but I want to leave the country and the sooner I go the better for all concerned.

The letter was signed 'Cosmo Brown'.

The recipient went straight to the police and under their instructions and observation met the writer, who was promptly arrested. In court the prisoner, who had an honourable army record, expressed regret for what he had done and affirmed the accusation in the letter was an absolute invention. It was stated that he had been wounded by a piece of shrapnel and this was the reason for his sending blackmailing letters.

The unsubstantiated nature of the accusation may well have been one strong reason for the prosecutor's willingness to report the letter immediately to the police. However, we have seen that neither the accuracy nor the substantive content of the allegedly discreditable information possessed by the blackmailer are the sole factors determining a response of co-operation or non-co-operation on the part of the victim. In other words, evasion of taxes, heterosexual promiscuity, homosexual interests, procurement of abortion, bigamous marriage, occupational incompetence, and all the rest of the practices blackmailers have seen fit to profit out of over the years, are patently not the root cause of the offence. Common to all is the unifying element of the *reaction of some others* to news that someone has deviated from a norm: the events which scandalise us vary, and whether a reaction to imputed deviance is positive, negative, or one of supreme indifference, is dependent on a complex range of contingencies. The well-publicised connection between espionage, blackmail, and sexual deviance pertains because in some situations the betrayal of state secrets proves more acceptable to the victim than the anticipated revelation of otherwise harmless preferences to a specific audience of fellow patriots. The victim's fear of stigmatisation strengthens the bargaining power of the blackmailer and leads to a major offence.[28]

A scandal can be a private and a public affair. Repercussions for the life of someone on the receiving end of moral condemnation vary in severity according to the extent to which his reputation is identifiable with the group interests he represents. The blackmailer can, therefore, threaten to transmit information to three major categories of external assessors:

(1)   formal public agents of social control, e.g. the police;
(2)   the mass media;
(3)   private audiences (a host of people, ranging from immediate friends, relations and colleagues, through to corporate organisations

offering employment opportunities).[29]

No one would need to pay blackmail if his interests were not bound up with those of others; the problem is really one of determining the nature of such interests, how they can be separated out, and what they tell us about the substantive organisation of society. Earlier we noted that respectability is linked to reputation by virtue of a series of ideologies of moral worth: those most vulnerable to blackmail are the very people exhibiting the greatest commitment to the predominant moral order.[30] Victims appearing in court — and presumably many others — are particularly susceptible on account of their psycho-social investment in 'good reputation'; taken all in all we can describe this major category as vulnerable careerists.

Vulnerable careerists are essentially dependent careerists; as F.G. Bailey has indicated, 'breaking the rules matters most when one is also letting the side down'.[31] Blackmail victims pay because they are afraid of the consequences for *some phase* in their career of the revelation of information they *believe* may bring about the scandalised withdrawal of approval, and possibly social exclusion. In this context, the concept of career is not limited to occupation, and refers to universal aspects of one's life project. An example from the nineteenth century adds a useful illustration:

A doctor had been threatened with accusations of an 'infamous crime' with intent to extort ten shillings; sentencing the offender, a painter, the judge commended the equity of the jury's verdict:[32]

> it would have been a scandal to justice if they had come to any other conclusion. There was no doubt that the prisoner found himself in communication with a gentleman who was kind enough to give him money to enable him to go to the hospital. There was no doubt whatever also that the prisoner then conceived the horrid idea of extorting money from him by threatening to accuse him of an unnatural offence. The crime was a very bad one when it was committed against anyone, but when it was committed against a medical man, whose whole life and fortune depended on maintaining a good character, especially for morality, such a charge might simply blast him. He [Mr Justice Field] had known several medical men to have succumbed to the attacks of such people as the prisoner. To attempt to levy money by blackmail, by threatening to accuse a gentleman of such an odious offence must be marked with great severity, and he sentenced the prisoner to 10 years penal servitude.

Overall changes in the organisation of our society since the 'Age of Scandal' have transformed workaday human lives into careers, pulled into shape by the differential strains and stresses transmitted along the golden chains of the cash nexus. Members of society are vulnerable careerists, not because they are necessarily ambitious, but because they wish to have and to hold whatever benefits they see themselves possessing. The concept of vulnerable career corresponds with the twin features of respectability mentioned earlier: a pattern of evaluated interaction with others, during the course of which judgments may be passed on the bases of generally legitimated ideologies of moral worth. The relationship of the blackmailer to the victim is one where both parties simultaneously claim respectable roles and reputations; audience reaction to a discovered transaction of this kind will be determined by concealed or manifest strains or pressures in the overall system of socio-economic relations.

Questions of whether behaviour is privately or publicly immoral cannot be answered by looking closely at the nature of the conduct in question (e.g. homosexuality, tax evasion), but rather at the pressures constraining certain people at a certain time to interpret these behaviours as threatening to their interests. All vulnerability is therefore circumstantial vulnerability, and three broad categories should be distinguished.

(1)   Members of certain occupational groups are especially vulnerable because of the delicate nature of their work. Professional organisations sometimes demand unyielding obedience from their members to prescribed standards of conduct. Professional rules of conduct can extend well beyond claims to the unique possession of valued knowledge and competence: 'Priests, doctors (and others who attend to people's health) and lawyers recognise the necessity of maintaining these standards by submitting themselves to the discipline enforced by their own courts, some of which are Statutory Tribunals, exercising quasi-judicial authority'.[33] From the occasional reported proceedings of these professional disciplinary bodies we know great care is taken, when the reputation of an individual member is under attack, that all enquiries are organised and publicly presented to show to best advantage the integrity of the professional group as a whole. However unintentionally, this approach assists the group to maintain its claim to a privileged position since the nature and function of official morality — by which we mean codes of moral behaviour prescribed as awesomely legitimate and binding — is to preserve group solidarity in the face of anticipated attacks from 'outsiders' who may or may not accept the status quo.[34]

Control of information over the self by members — self-control — advertises a rightful claim to control the lives of others and to judge them worthy or unworthy. These groups are composed of people who are socialised or professionalised into the maintenance of compartmentalised lives — calculated skills are required to retain the integrity of these spheres and to know where to draw the line between

enterprise was May Churchill, who has passed into history as 'Chicago May' (described in the 1920s as 'the worst woman in the world'). In 1907 she was known to the police as 'one of the most notorious women in London, whose chief business was to compromise and blackmail men'.[40]

The 'badger game' is, of course, practised with varying degrees of persistence and skill and it arises within a variety of contexts. For example an unemployed man tried recently to advertise his wife's availability to other men on reasonable terms, in a magazine. Arrangements were made for a respondent to spend an evening with the wife yet the following day her husband phoned the client, posing as cruelly wronged, and demanding money on threat of exposure. In court he pleaded guilty, but it was offered in his defence that he had only sought the money in compensation for his wife's newly aroused attachment to the other man.

Examples of the 'badger game' are plentiful in the literature. They commonly emerge from the blackmailer's conspiracy to create information in the light of which the victim may hopefully be persuaded his public reputation can be reconstructed to his disadvantage.

(2)   Opportunistic blackmail

Bearing from the blackmailer's viewpoint, the hallmark of serendipity; the unexpected discovery of discreditable information which he believes can be transformed into cash. A conjunction between unemployment and the discovery of a wallet, diary, passport, or other article of personal property containing information which appears at first blush indicative of some 'guilty secret' has led to several criminal prosecutions. One prisoner affirmed, 'I thought I could blackmail him to get some money because I was hard up'. Should the information discovered turn out to all intents and purposes devoid of any scandal-bearing quality, an enterprising offender may find it expedient to embellish the contents with socially credible imputations of deviance: A labourer pleaded guilty to sending a letter demanding £40 from 'Mr A'; prosecuting counsel[41]

> said that whilst 'Mr A' and his wife were canoeing on the river Wey the boat capsized and they were thrown in the water. On returning to Guildford 'Mr A' found he had lost his wallet which contained three photographs and a letter. The letter was from 'Mr A's' wife written to him before their marriage. The labourer wrote to 'Mr A' saying that he had found the wallet floating in

the river and asked £40 for the article. 'Mr A' went straight to the police and the defendant was arrested.

(3)   Commercial research

This follows from the planned pursuit of commercially viable information — allegedly one trade-mark of the master blackmailer. Recently, the Younger Committee on Privacy stressed certain dangers of accumulating large amounts of personal information in data banks, thus opening the lives of private citizens, entitled to some protection, to possibly invidious scrutiny.[42] A case the Committee did not mention occurred during the Second World War when two young men employed at the Air Ministry were accused of using official information as the basis for writing to certain vulnerable people outlining the possible consequences of exposure, and offering — for a fee — to destroy the documentary evidence. The stimulus behind these criminal threats appears to have been a collection of anonymous letters forwarded to a government department.

(4)   Participant blackmail

Participant blackmail differs from the other three forms in so far as it arises out of a pre-existing relationship between the blackmailer and the victim. In all such instances, blackmail is an extension of previous interaction, where threatening behaviour of this more explicit type apparently played no part.

In the famous Carbon Paper case 'high pressure selling methods' were said to have engineered employees, responsible for buying office stationery, into accepting large-scale deliveries of unnecessary carbon paper. Under pressure from the salesman to settle the account, some trusted workers embezzled the firm's money, not for their own use, but to pay off their persistent creditors and so cover up their mistakes. One woman in the Midlands, described as a 'loyal and trusted employee with a golden character', took delivery of carbon paper worth £7000 from three firms, and forged the managing director's signature to pay for it. Fortunately this person was granted a conditional discharge by the court.[43]

Another common form of participant blackmail has its origins in sexual intimacy. After tiring of a sexual association with a destitute man for whom she had found work, an elderly welfare worker found herself the recipient of demanding letters, one of which contained the line, 'The price of silence is £200. Australia indicated'. She sought police help and on sentencing the man responsible to fifteen months in prison, the recorder informed him, 'you bit the hand that fed you, and you tried to make capital out of a situation which you helped to create, and which you knew would be one of intolerable shame to this lady, and bring disaster to her life and the life of her husband'.[44]

The complex relationship developing between the blackmailer and his victim is responsive to the four types of general situation previously outlined. These relations in turn have repercussions for the way the blackmailer himself approaches the transaction, and the wider social significance of the information he shares with his victim. Hence, the despised role of moral murderer is not simply the product of a pre-existing pathological state of mind, but one which develops differentially during the course of everyday living, sharing its own situated moral burden with those immediately involved.

Chapter 5

Blackmail as a Social Relationship

Only in the public drama that surrounds the criminal law are we presented with an image of the credibility of justice.

Richard Quinney[1]

Outside works of fiction,[2] recorded accounts of the negotiations between the blackmailer and his victim are rare. Here is one exception:

Case VIII (exploratory negotiation)   At Sheffield in 1898 a solicitor received a letter from, it was eventually revealed, a twenty-six-year-old foreign correspondent. The opening gambit read:

> The object of the present is to inform you that I know of your having committed bigamy. You, no doubt, are aware of the nature of the consequences which would follow if this your secret were let out. I am intending to go out to Africa and shall require £300, and as I have only £50 all told I am short of £250, and shall if you can make it convenient and let me have this sum in way of remuneration for keeping your secret from other people. You will kindly send the money in the shape of 25 Bank of England £10 notes.

The recipient, taking up the invitation, replied:

> I have received your letter, in reply I wish to say that I am prepared to negotiate for settlement with you if you will let me know the lowest amount you will take to keep quiet on the matter. Please communicate with me again by the same means.

To which, in turn, the prisoner answered:

> Reply to yours of today's date I note your willingness to negotiate on the pending matter and wish me to state the lowest figure. As I

already mentioned to you I require £250 to enable me to carry out
my intention and will be glad to have your offer, as no doubt you
will be able to gauge better the value of the secret than I myself.
As for my part, I think £250 a very reasonable figure since you can
well afford it, and I am almost in a desperate position, or else you
may feel assured, I should never have troubled. Being greatly in
need of money I shall be extremely obliged to you if you will send
me, say £30 — £40 on receipt of this to the given address, as part
payment of the sum to be defined yet. I give you my word of
honour that I shall not breathe it to anybody if you will only be
kind enough and help me out of my desperate position, and if
perchance I shall have luck out yonder in Africa I promise you
every penny back. Trusting to have your good news with
remittance.

The address was given as 'GPO, Sheffield'
    By return of post, a face-to-face encounter was suggested:
    I received your letter yesterday morning, and if you will meet me
    outside the General Post Office (Haymarket) tomorrow, Monday
    night, at 8 o'clock we can adjourn somewhere to talk over matters
    and arrange a settlement. You have the advantage of knowing me,
    so I shall wait for you to make yourself known. In the meantime
    I trust you to keep quiet.

The appointment was kept, the would-be blackmailer arrested and
later prosecuted at Leeds Assizes.
    On behalf of the defence it was argued the accused must have
written the letters as a practical joke (a not infrequent explanation
on the first cause of a blackmail transaction). The charge of bigamy
was unfounded. He was earning about £5 a week and therefore did
not need money; furthermore he had no real intention of going to
Africa. The prisoner's employer attested to his character and said
he was quite willing to have him back; anyone knowing the
accused, counsel went so far as to state, would appreciate the
frivolity of the charge. Unimpressed, the judge imprisoned the
offender for six months with hard labour: 'some people on receipt of
such letters would have been so terrorised that they might have
commenced to make payments, and perhaps have continued to do so
for the rest of their lives'.[3]

Many of the cases coming before the courts only arrive there because
the blackmailer's invitation to negotiate has elicited a negative response
from the other party. Alternatively, after paying at least once, the
victim will have gone to the police and reported what he takes to be

an offence. Which ever of these variants applies, very often the police find it necessary to stage an observed transaction in order to obtain adequate evidence for a conviction — a fair cop. Deliberately manipulated negotiations transform attempted into completed blackmail: the first stage in the transformation of the moral status of the offender from that of unknown private citizen, attempting to make a few pounds on the side (or some similar variant), into a publicly stigmatised 'blackmailer'. It is a form of 'status passage' — a road along which the designated blackmailer is an unwilling traveller.[4]

This does not mean blackmail is uncompleted unless the police witness the transaction; it means that until the police obtain reproducible evidence for a court prosecution, the behaviour is not officially labelled 'criminal blackmail' and may, therefore, not be recognised as such. Police involvement with complainants is the first stage in the process of selecting out certain ingredients in the transaction to correspond with the stereotype of blackmail. These ingredients are parsimoniously defined in law as 'demanding money with menaces'.

So far, our discussion of blackmail has largely been confined to one perspective only: that of the victim, as interpreted by outraged society through the blackmail stereotype. However we have observed that blackmail transactions can be distinguished in terms of at least four major situational factors. An examination of the reported justifications at hand to assist the *detected blackmailer* explain his actions and to allocate responsibility for his part in the affair, both before the police and the courts, will enhance our appreciation of the situated nature of the offence.

Explanations offered by blackmailers, are variously recorded at five points in the transaction:

(1)   at the time of the transaction, or prior to the offence;

(2)   on arrest or after arrest, and prior to court proceedings;

(3)   during court proceedings under examination and cross-examination;

(4)   by the defendant or by others after the trial has concluded;

(5)   in the Court of Appeal (where they may be confirmed or denied).

Justificatory statements appearing in these situations probably vary widely but the available evidence is insufficient to detail all variations. One overall constraining factor is the legal definition of the anti-social nature of demanding money with menaces. When legal dispute is at a minimum, that is when the behaviour with which a defendant is charged falls clearly within the meaning of the criminal legislation (either in term of the nature of the demand itself of the threat to reputation), extra-legal pleas of justification become essential. The necessary preoccupation of the law with 'the worst cases' (i.e. in effect usually those apparently closest to the stereotype of 'true blackmail'), means that when a person is charged and prosecuted for blackmail he has to find explanations for what has happened in terms of the situation described to him by his accusers underscoring the illegality and unworthiness of his actions. In this connection the following exchange from the transcript of the 'Mr A Case' is of interest.[5]

Question:	'Are you a man absolutely devoid both of honesty and honour? '
Answer:	'No.'
Question:	'Have you honesty? '
Answer:	'Yes.'
Question:	'And honour? '
Answer:	'Amongst my friends, yes.'
Question:	'Well, we will investigate it a little. First of all, we will take the question of honesty. In fact have you not been living on blackmail practically all your life? (a pause). Do you say, "Yes"?'
Answer:	'I do not say "Yes". No.'
Question:	'How many people have you blackmailed? '
Answer:	'Nobody, and it won't help you at all to bully me either, I may say.'
Question:	'How many people have you blackmailed? '
Answer:	'Nobody.'

In response to these sorts of pressures, explanations offered by accused blackmailers hover around a range of socially approved justificatory statements: 'accounts in which one accepts responsibility for the act in question, but denies the pejorative quality associated with it.'[6] Apologies, therefore, should not be confused with justifications. Apologies 'represent a splitting of the self into a blameworthy part that stands back and sympathises with the blame giving, and, by implication is worthy of being brought back into the fold.'[7]

Circumstances also combine to help offenders justify their conduct to others: in other words, they can agree with the law that blackmail is wrong since they are not 'really' blackmailers.[8]

For maximum efficacy, justifications need to be couched in language which others will recognise and hopefully find acceptable — they must draw upon a familiar vocabulary of motivations. For this reason the accused, or his counsel, is bound to proffer some explanation of what has taken place which will suggest a socially approved motive underlies an apparently criminal act. In all cases the defendant is confronted with a situation where he is described as the author of the offence; but he himself may represent his actions as an integral feature of an on-going, and frequently legitimate, social relationship. The meaning of such interaction will depend upon the extent to which the disapproved transaction has developed from some form of prior association, where a degree of familiarity involving both parties was inescapable. Rephrasing this in terms of the Theft Act 1968, the putative blackmailer will set out to demonstrate that he *believed* he had a right to the money he claimed, and to ask for it in the way he did.

Sometimes justifications of blackmail work. A lance-corporal, charged with sending letters to a doctor threatening to accuse him of 'a certain crime', was found guilty but with a strong recommendation to mercy from the jury on account of his youth and ignorance of the law. The implication behind this case was that the soldier had a grievance against the doctor but resorted to illegal means to obtain what he thought were his rights. Apparently he was under the impression he could obtain compensation from the doctor, presumably for damages he felt he could have recovered in a court of law. The recorder told him he was not to blame for fighting out the case until the bitter end as he had wished to bring his version of the story before the jury. However, blackmail was wrong and judges rarely refrained from sending a blackmailer to penal servitude; in recognition of the circumstances it was decided to keep him in custody until the first day of the next Sessions and then bind him over in token demonstration that no punishment had been passed on him.[9]

When, a year later in 1935, a property dealer was found guilty at Hampshire Assizes of sending four blackmailing letters, the jury entered a strong recommendation to mercy in view of the fact 'that the prisoner was underpaid'. The victim, who was the defendant's former employer, had previously been sentenced to five years' penal servitude for false pretences and forgery. The threats were to reveal his malpractice. Thus one letter which had been sent to the victim, prior to his imprisonment, included the statement: 'Unless you can see your way to send the money to my mother by tomorrow, I shall take my own steps to show up your delinquencies in dealing with clients' money.' Three other letters were read in court, one concluded: 'To protect myself I sent a sealed packet addressed to the Law Society to a friend to be forwarded if anything happens.'

Defence counsel argued that blackmail was not conclusively proved since the tone of the letters indicated the writer was requesting a loan and help. Nothing more. With all this going for him the defendant received a sentence of fifteen months' imprisonment with hard labour.[10]

To gain some sympathy for his actions the accused must take care to show that he feels he has some entitlement to open a business transaction. That although he *may* know he is involved in strictly extra-legal activity, he is so involved because of the peculiar situation in which he finds himself where others, now sitting in judgment, would behave in a similar fashion. Threatened with stereotyping as a blackmailer, he is struggling to sustain 'a definition of himself as a "normal" person'.[11] One of the only techniques open to him when he reaches the courtroom — since the evidence is patently weighted against him — is to fall back on a stock series of justificatory 'accounts', hopefully mediating in some way between himself, a severe sentence, and exposure to public degradation.

Analysis of reports of criminal proceedings yields a recurring range of justifications offered by the alleged blackmailer to account for his actions and to disavow criminal intent:[12]

(1)	Commercial entitlement	Relations
(2)	Relational entitlement	of
(3)	Service provision	exchange
(4)	Compensatory	
(5)	Restitutive	Social justice
(6)	Vengeful	
(7)	Moral crusade	Personally pressurising
(8)	Blackmail under threat	situations

Whether they are recorded in letters representing an integral feature of the transaction at the time, or reported statements made as a prosecution progresses, justifications for blackmail tend to fall into three major categories: relations of exchange, social justice and personally pressurising situations. They represent an index of the *situational pressures* to which blackmailers feel they can credibly claim to be responding whilst negotiating the transaction; or after the event, when occupying the place of the judged. Further, they represent the claim that far from being an isolable, unilaterally initiated evil, blackmail is above all a social relationship reflecting taken for granted features of everyday life.

(1) Relations of exchange

Exchange is a central mechanism of social life. The blackmailer, no less than other members of the community, acts in response to these assumptions: he does not believe he is getting something for nothing — he is not a thief. On the contrary, he is entitled to ask for some return in consideration of favours rendered in the past and services to come in the future. That the law may not approve of such transactions is hardly relevant since, as everyone knows, a great deal of everyday social life involves legally proscribed activities. By offering something in return for cash payments the blackmailer can successfully demonstrate to himself, and hopefully to others, that he is not making an undue demand nor is he taking any reprehensible advantage of the victim.

Sometime public prosecutor Sir Richard Muir was occasionally called upon by public men to hush up threatening scandals. One 'sensational case of blackmail' apparently involved a notable MP, who called upon Muir to negotiate the matter privately on his behalf. 'In the result some thousands of pounds were paid to buy off the bloodsuckers and', remarks the biographer, 'when I say that had he not done so the MP might have gone to penal servitude for five years it will probably be thought that the money was well spent.'[13]

W.R. Harrison of the Home Office Forensic Science Laboratory has provided a recipe for the ideal and potentially successful blackmail letter.[14]

To be taken seriously it should be identifiable in terms of the following characteristics:

(1)   the sum of money demanded should be calculated according to the capacity of the victim to pay.

(2)   there should be practicable instructions specifying the way in which money is to pass from the victim to the blackmailer.

(3)   the genuine blackmailing letter should contain 'a hint, if nothing more definite' of some reason why the victim should be called upon to pay. 'This almost invariably takes the form of the writer assuming a nauseating hypocritically moral tone, rebuking the recipient either for some form of sexual delinquency or for an evasion of income tax, which the writer feels should be punished by the extortion of money, to be regarded by the victim as a well-merited fine for the offence.'

Drawing on his forensic experience, Harrison notes that the writer may further seek to justify his actions by:

(1)   relating a story of personal misfortune.

(2)   stating that he intends to regard the payment as a loan.

(3)   attempting to impress on his victims that the demands must not be considered as blackmail but merely a request for assistance.

(4)   threatening certain consequences if the victim fails to keep silent.

(5)   promising that this demand is the last.

Apart from generally oversimplifying the issue, an important point that Harrison does not make is that letters written by blackmailers give us insight into the immediate social meanings of the proposed transaction, tinged with the element of sophistication hinted by the biographer of Sir Richard Muir.

Case IX (mass blackmail)   Three brothers, Richard, Leonard and Edward Chrimes were proved to have circulated on 6 October 1898 a letter to between eight and ten thousand women:

Madame, I am in possession of letters of yours by which I can positively prove that you did on or about — commit, or attempt to commit the fearful crime of abortion by preventing or attempting to prevent yourself giving birth to a child. Either of these constitutes a criminal act punishable by penal servitude and legal proceedings have already been commenced against you, and your immediate arrest will be effected unless you send me on or before Tuesday morning next the sum of £2. 2/-. being costs already incurred by me, and your solemn promise on oath before God that never again by whatsoever means will you prevent or attempt to prevent yourself giving birth to a child. No notice whatsoever will be taken of your letter unless postal orders (cheques, stamps etc. will not be accepted) for the above amount are enclosed and received by me on the aforesaid day. Failing to comply with these two requests, you will be immediately arrested without further warning. All legal proceedings will be stopped on receipt of the £2. 2/-. and the incriminating documents . . . will be returned to you and you will hear nothing further of the matter.

I am, Madame etc.

(signed) Charles J. Mitchell, Public Official.

One reply to this offer ran:

Oct. 11th, 1898. Dear Sir — I am very sorry I have done wrong. I did not know I had done wrong to myself or any one else and, as regards trying to prevent myself from being confined, I do not know that ever I have done so, for the girl that you are alluding to is a big, fine girl, as healthy as any child could be, and is eight months old; and I do not call that doing away with the babe, or trying to do so. But if I have done wrong I ask you to forgive me, as I did not know I was doing wrong. I will promise that I will never do wrong any more, for Christ's sake. Amen.

The name of the writer, who seems to have acted under the belief that some kind of all-seeing eye was fixed upon her, was not disclosed in court when the letter was read. It contained two guineas. Towards the end of the trial at the Old Bailey, Mr Justice Hawkins said he could not conceive of a more convincing letter showing belief in the threats and terror lest the threats be put into operation. 'There were thousands of letters of that character', he states, quoting from a further reply from a servant girl saying that she did not think she was pregnant but did not wish her mistress to know of her fears in case she would lose her situation.

He also referred to the role of legal prohibitions in strengthening the blackmailer's hand:

the charge which was made against the prisoners was one of the most serious known to our criminal law. It was one which affected the happiness and the comfort, and he might also say the safety, of every human being in this country, because, beyond all question, to write to a man or a woman threatening to charge a criminal offence which might by law, although it was discretion with the Judge, be visited with penal servitude for life, was calculated to create terror and alarm to those to whom the threats were made; and where it was endeavoured to extort money by means of those threats it amounted to no less than robbery of the worst description if those monies were obtained.

As a consequence Edward and Richard Chrimes received twelve years penal servitude each. Leonard, the younger of the brothers, was sentenced to penal servitude for seven years. In the words of E.S. Turner, 'ten thousand wives breathed freely again'.[15]

Prosecuting counsel stated that large-scale gains had been calculated in this scheme. The brothers originally published thinly disguised advertisements for abortifacients passing under the trade name of 'Lady Montroses Miraculous Female Tabules' — ('acknowledged by ladies throughout the world to be worth a guinea per tabule'). Advertisements for the tabules and later for another product of a similar nature 'Panolia', brought in shoals of replies. Accumulating these gave the prisoners the names and addresses of 12,000 women who thought themselves pregnant and wanted to be rid of the child.

To avoid identification the letter offering the services of 'Charles J Mitchell, Public Official' was composed with great care and ingenuity. Three envelopes were involved: an outer envelope, and immediately inside that another on which there was a request that if the letter was undelivered it should be returned to 'Mitchell.' Enclosed was a third printed envelope to be used for communication with 'Mitchell'.

A warehouseman, William Clifford, brought the original prosecution. He said his wife had not known when she sent for the tabules whether she was pregnant or not — she believed she was not, but was confined eight months later. (The chemist who had innocently made up the tabules said in court that they were quite harmless.) When the letter from 'Mitchell' reached the Clifford household, William Clifford opened it and took it straight to the police. From that point onwards the brothers Crimes were under police surveillance.

Once informed about this matter the police intercepted 1,785 letters going back to the self-styled public official. Of these 413 contained money. There was no doubt that the prisoners were guilty as charged: the evidence was overwhelmingly against them and the defence could do little by way of justification. Only one brother, Richard, was ultimately to plead not guilty to blackmail.[16] None of the accused pleaded moral crusade yet the burden of their threat stirred a responsive chord in many a recipient's heart.

Opportunities for blackmail are clearly enmeshed within our social system. What is important too, as the Wolfenden Report noted in connection with legislation against male homosexuality, is that accusations of secretly deviant activity do not need to have an objective reference point in criminal law.

Whatever the accusation the conduct of the blackmailer is implicitly 'justified' in so far as he may consider it appropriate to seek a source of income from activities law *or custom* have labelled deviant.[17] The willingness of relatively well-reputed papers and journals to carry advertisements of the kind capitalised by the brothers Chrimes forged an important link in their chain of entrepreneurial activities. The foreman of the jury finding Richard Chrimes guilty added a collective rider to the verdict:[18]

> The jury feel that such a vile plot, even with all the ingenuity
> displayed in it, could only have been possible by the acceptance
> of such immoral advertisement by a section of the Press —
> religious and secular — well knowing their nature. The jury further
> expressed their earnest conviction that means should be found to
> suppress such advertisements and the institutions from which
> they emanate, as they consider them direct incentives to ignorant
> and evil minded women to commit crime.

Our previous distinction between attempted and completed blackmail comes in again here. So-called victims, the blackmailer may argue, refuse to negotiate if they are confident of their status and reputation in society. Those people who complete the transaction do so because they have something to lose and therefore something to gain. Equally, the blackmailer can suggest he offers a social service to the wider community through his readiness to enter into a conspiracy to preserve the façade of outward respectability.

Realising that life in the beauty culture business[19] offered up particular possibilities amidst the prudery and disapproval of cosmetics in mid-Victorian London, Rachel Leverson opened a Beauty Parlour at 47a New Bond Street. Her well-chosen slogan was 'Beautiful for Ever'.[20] Like the brothers Chrimes she used innocuous and inexpensive chemicals as the basis for her entrepreneurial activity. Elizabeth Jenkins's description of her at this time is not without interest:[21]

> The extraordinary being had not, at first glance, the appearance

one would expect of a beauty specialist. She was tall, corpulent and bold-featured, and, though richly dressed, had no pretensions to beauty of her own. She was in fact both formidable and repellent, but the effect she created in the weaker minds of her clients was the more powerful. They received the impression that here was a woman of supernormal abilities.

In her lavishly decorated 'Temple of Beauty' she charged ageing and wealthy women vast prices for ineffective and certainly inexpensive beauty preparations. She also managed to attract a reputation as someone who would not restrain herself from stooping to blackmail. Her strong appeal was specifically to women who felt their attractions were fading and wanted to arrest the process. When clients discovered they had paid outrageous prices for ineffective 'remedial' beauty treatment and threatened exposure, Rachel Leverson, would explicitly hold before them the spectacle of the open ridicule of a society which found ugly women a source of amusement, especially those who tried to alter 'nature' or hold the passage of time at arm's length. Above all, Rachel Leverson could threaten to make her recalcitrant clients look 'improper' in the eyes of the world.

She was eventually prosecuted when she pushed one of her clients too far and was sentenced to penal servitude for five years on a charge of obtaining £600 by false pretences; and with conspiring to obtain various other sums totalling £1,400 from a widow, Mrs Borrodaile, who had been parted from her money under the impression that Rachel Leverson was arranging a marriage between herself and Lord Ranelagh. Released from prison on ticket-of-leave in 1872 she recommenced business in another part of London and was soon making money. Following a second appearance at the Old Bailey in 1878 she died in Woking prison ten years later.

The fact that the price for a particular service is extortionate does not mean a service is not provided, Rachel Leverson, like many undramatic blackmailers since, claimed to be fulfilling a public need. Blackmailers claiming to offer a service explicitly deny their actions are grounded totally in self-interest; a process of exchange has taken place. Very often their offer to preserve someone's reputation is not restricted to the exercise of restraint over publication, they also offer to return evidence of their client's lapse:

Case X (service blackmail)

Dear Sir — I have purchased from one of the books barrows in Farringdon Street an album which may be of interest to you. It contains portraits of the chief authors in the Parnell Commission,

including that of the vendor of the Piggott forgeries. It is also a
series of cuttings from 'United Ireland', giving some particulars of
his blackballing twice at the Atheneum Club. The price I ask for
this book is £100 for which I will undertake to destroy it. If you
do not care to have it, I shall forward it as a present to the editor
of the 'Swiss and Nice Times' who will doubtless make good copy
out of it. It will be despatched to Mr Webb on Saturday next by
the midday mail.

Yours faithfully.

Quoted at Bow Street police court in March 1899, the letter had been
received in Nice by the editor of a paper, the 'Riviera Daily'. This man
who had formerly been a leading member of the Conservative party in
Ireland, was instrumental in bringing to light facts leading to the
Parnell Commission, thereby incurring the hostility of the Nationalist
Party. It was said in court that he was the person referred to in the
letter: at one time his father had been deputy governor at the
Marchalsea Prison in Dublin and a story had been circulated that he
himself had been a warder there. Counsel for the prosecution stated
the recipient had never been blackballed by the Athenaeum and had
never been a candidate at that club.

The writer offering first refusal of his 'find', was a London journalist
who had worked for the potential victim for a short time before being
dismissed for drunkenness. On his arrest the police found a letter in his
possession addressed to the French Minister of War containing accusations
against the victim which, if believed, it was suggested, would have
entirely ruined his whole career as a journalist in France.

Trapped, the attempted blackmailer wrote a letter of apology read out
by defence counsel:

Acting on your advice and feeling its accuracy, I hereby tender my
most sincere and hearty apology for sending such an uncalled for
letter . . . Such a letter everybody knows could not have been written
by me in my sane moments and Mr — will thoroughly appreciate the
state of mind which produced such a letter. In fact, the horrible
anxiety and worry to which I have been subjected since my return
from France — I have been suffering also from want of food, and
doubtless that has produced an effect upon my nerves which caused
me some mental abberration. The mere fact that other communications
of a similar nature were written by me is another demonstration of
my condition of mind at the time. I hope, therefore, that Mr — will,
under the circumstances, accept my apology, which I hereby heartily
tender.

I am, Yours faithfully, . . .

On behalf of the defence it was stated the victim had published an accusation of drunkenness against the prisoner in a London newspaper. After having written the above penitent letter, the prosecution informed the court that the prisoner in the cells after the previous day's trial, said he would try to ruin the prosecutor; he felt very strongly the imputations against him of drunkenness which he thought could ruin his career. He had also asserted that he would being an action against the recipient for defamation of character and false imprisonment.

In the event the apology worked. Rather unusually, it was accepted on the basis of assurances there would be no further repetition of the offence and the prisoner was discharged on a surety of £100 promising the magistrate to guard his language in the future.[22]

Closely akin to service provision, is the justification of commercial entitlement. The distinction between the two lies in the nature of the relationship between the individuals concerned prior to an accusation of blackmail. Whereas service blackmail is frequently associated with some form of disreputable activity (illicit sex, drug use, gambling, etc.), the category commercial entitlement denotes particularly those actions which the accused himself sees arising out of a previous *legitimate* commercial claim.

'Thorne Motor Trade Association and Another, 1937',[23] was a classic case of alleged blackmail arising out of what many considered to be legitimate business practice — the use of the 'stop list'. The Motor Trade Association had been partly formed as a price maintenance agency to keep a watchful eye over the price of cars sold by members and non-members. If any dealer sold a car at less than list price the Association could place him on the 'stop list', thus refusing to send him further supplies and thereby jeopardising his business. Because this was seen as a rather drastic technique of economic control, dealers pleading mitigating circumstances were allowed to pay a fine to prevent their names being placed on the 'list'. The Thorne affair was described in law as a 'friendly' case. A member of the association sought a declaration by the courts that the use of the stop list as a means to collect money was illegal and constituted demanding money with menaces under section 29 (1) (i) of the Theft Act, 1916. It was held by the House of Lords that the rule was not illegal if operated with the honest intention of carrying out the trade policy of the association 'in which case the association would not be demanding the payment without reasonable or probable cause'.[24]

Commenting on the legal aspects of the case, Smith and Hogan observe:[25]

Both Lord Atkin and Lord Wright were expressly of the opinion that a trade association demanding money as the price of not putting a trader on its stop list, thereby cutting off the trader's supply of goods from members of the association, would be demanding with menaces, although it might not be blackmail if the association were acting lawfully in threatening to put the trader on its stop list *and* the price demanded were not unreasonable having regard to the legitimate business interests of the association.

As these critics later remark, the problem with blackmail is not 'merely one of classification'. It is 'to draw the line between demands for property which are legitimate and demands which amount to blackmail'. They further note that 'it is not possible to categorise demands in advance of the circumstances'.[26]

Case XI (commercial entitlement)   Although the following example does not involve threats against reputation, the melodramatic letter quoted (affording us interesting insight into how one person with a grievance apparently thought a blackmail letter would look), arose out of a previous business transaction of a conventional kind. Ultimately the defendant was found not-guilty, partly following conflicting evidence from handwriting experts as to the authorship of the letter.

The defendant, a farmer, had mortgaged his property and when the mortgagees foreclosed he asked the victim to buy the property for him in the sale, promising him to repay him shortly. Repayment was not forthcoming and after two years the victim sold part of the property; consequently the writer of the letter acted, under the impression the victim had profited to the extent of £300, which he wanted to get back. To this end, it was alleged by the prosecution at Exeter Assizes in 1899, the accused wrote the victim a letter:

Headquarters Socialistic Commune, London.
We have carefully investigated and considered this matter, and this is our decision. Within seven days of your receipt of this you shall pay to him the sum of £300 in Bank of England notes addressed to him at Haytor View, Moretonhampstead, with the intimation that he shall leave the country within three months and not further molest you, and please make this clear to him, as he knows nothing of this. And in case you fail to do this, prepare to meet your doom, as you and your agent Loveys will be at once removed, and do not think you will escape, as our funds are ample and our organisation is perfect the world over. The hand that takes this to you is deputed to carry out our commands, therefore herein fail not. And if (the writer) fails to carry out his part we shall at once remove him and protect you — ALPHA, Chairman and Secretary.

A newspaper cutting was enclosed:

> This extraordinary man, by means of an array of spies and agents, commands a vast organization which underlies and controls the visible movement of all secret societies upon earth, and whose unseen presence pervades the whole of European and American society through all its stages, from an Imperial court or a presidential reputation to the meeting of a trade union executive or a secret conclave of anarchists and outcasts from the pale of respectable society.

Two weeks after its receipt the writer was arrested at Plymouth. He suggested that someone must have sent the letter as a hoax with the intention of doing him an injury. Before the magistrates he steadfastly denied having sent the letter though the complainant said he recognised the handwriting.[27]

A final variation on the theme of exchange is relational entitlement. Here blackmailers define the situation as one where, because of a past association, they are entitled to press for some financial return. Requests or demands of this nature may receive further legitimation when the victim apparently occupies an advantageous socio-economic position.

One 'elderly gentleman' prosecuted his bankrupt nephew for couching his financial needs in somewhat pressing terms:

> Unless a sum you promised to refund of my legacy is paid to me you may expect my presence at Tyler's Green, when you will then and there have to appear before all the villagers and answer my complaint, and, moreover, make an ample apology for insulting my wife, who is vastly your superior, if not I will soundly horsewhip you before the villagers.

The complainant had loaned over £800 to his nephew; finding him reluctant to repay the money, he proceeded against him in the civil courts. The legacy at the heart of the matter had been left to his nephew by another uncle, most of the money passing to the complainant to help pay off the debt. Some time before the prosecution the defendant's wife called on his uncle and asked him to return money to his nephew; he refused to comply saying instead he would consider giving him a small part of the legacy. The magistrate committed the nephew for trial since he claimed he was officially powerless to handle the affair.[28]

Under certain circumstances, family disputes get out of control and pass into the criminal courts, and blackmail can be a family matter. My interviews with the police tended to confirm this was the experience of some detectives and is certainly a commonly shared belief. However, as far as the recorded cases are concerned, very few immediate family ties between blackmailer and victim have come to light, although there are a handful of other instances besides the one already quoted. In 1891 a theatrical manager was charged with sending a series of letters to his brother threatening exposure of some incident in his past life. But relational entitlement can constitute a much wider base for varying pressures than the one afforded by tortuous family connections; criminal blackmail is one outcome along this continuum.

Case XII (relational entitlement)   Knowing what we do about the subtle links between Victorian systems of class bound social relations and sexual morality, it comes as no surprise to find that a number of cases of blackmail originated from claims by self-proclaimed discarded mistresses and long lost 'natural' children. One such claim forced itself upon a wealthy MP in 1895. The claimant was a middle-aged man from Blackburn who insisted he was the victim's son. Prosecuting counsel stated the claim was impossible: a check on birth dates showed the victim was only twelve or fourteen at the time. The charge bringing the claimant before the Old Bailey, was threatening to publish a scandalous and defamatory libel with intent to extort money and not, as the prosecution stated might properly have been the case, demanding money with menaces.

The first letter received by the victim began with the words, 'Long lost dear father' and concluded, 'Your affectionate son', and the defendant gave the history of his family: his father had deserted his mother when he was a baby and was never seen again; his mother was now dead. 'I thought I had no father', he wrote, 'I should like the pleasure of seeing you, for I have not seen a father in my life'.

Several letters were then written variously signed 'Your enquiring son' and 'Your legitimate son'. Under the pressure of this correspondence the victim contacted the Chief Superintendant of Blackburn police to ask him to see the defendant; this was done and he promised not to repeat the annoyance. However the writing soon resumed and letters arrived signed 'Your determined son'. In one of these the author claimed he had the victim's photograph and would send him one of himself, which he did.

Gradually the letters changed their tone. The victim had steadfastly refused to accept the proposition put to him and on 22 August 1894 the defendant threatened to write to Henry Labouchère's 'Truth' and 'Reynold's' newspaper, exposing the scandalous way in which his putative father had neglected wife and family. On 18 September he wrote: 'If you don't come to some arrangement before long I can assure you it will not longer be kept a secret', and expressed a hope that the victim 'while in Paris was sleeping the sleep of the just'.

At this point the victim attempted to get his solicitor to see the defendant and to induce him to stop sending the letters. After the ensuing interview the defendant said he would never stop even if it cost him his life and began writing to the victim's wife addressing her as his 'dear step-mother'. The sole reason, said prosecuting counsel, for the institution of these criminal proceedings was a sense of annoyance. 'However idle the story might seem to them it was impossible to say what mischief might be done by such statements, especially when oft repeated in a public man's constituency.'

Letters had been received by the victim at Guildford, Brighton, and Paris. The persistent correspondent was, said the police, a hard-working and respectable man with a wife and two children. For the defence it was submitted that it had not been conclusively shown that the letters were sent with the intention of extorting money. The prisoner was mistaken in his ideas but he believed himself to be engaged in a laudable search for his long lost father. He had all along tried to avoid publicity, and every man was entitled to search for his father.

Upon a finding of 'guilty' the Common Serjeant observed that no apology had been offered by the prisoner and there had been no promise to abstain from these libels in the future. There seemed, he said, to be someone behind the prisoner who had some knowledge of law, although an imperfect knowledge, and care had been taken to frame the letters so that money was not expressly requested. Nevertheless, he felt, 'money was plainly what was required'. Defence counsel then interceded: he was instructed to say that the prisoner was sorry for what he had done and would undertake never in the future to circulate any such statements. The apology came too late and the guilty man left the court for a sentence of eighteen months' imprisonment with hard labour.[29]

(2) Social justice

Relations of exchange are distinguishable from those informed by notions of social justice in so far as the blackmailer chooses to emphasise his entitlement in terms of more general moral values. Turning to this second category we see that blackmailers have justified their behaviour by appealing to an ideology of justice incorporating compensation, restitution, and vengeance. This appeal is somewhat more abstract than the justification of exchange.

Let us take vengeance first:[30]

Even your correspondence and telegrams are in safe keeping. At

your every meeting you will be followed and watched. You shall
bitterly repent it. I am not to be trifled with. It is owing to you and
another that I am separated from my wife and my home broken up.
The other has paid the penalty and will show it to his dying day.
Your turn is to come in due course. Very well, you shall pay for it.

Letters of this kind are likely to emerge from prior associations. The
main difference between these and others in the category of exchange
rests with their emphasis on revenge rather than any other form of
entitlement.

At Bodmin Assizes a clerk admitted to having relieved the local vicar
of large sums of money through threats to inform the Bishop and to
take legal proceedings over the clergyman's alleged improprieties with
his wife: 'He was only too eager to hand it over to me. I had no need
of that which he pressed upon me'. In the dock the defendant told the
jury he felt justified in taking the money for revenge. The judge was
reported as saying:[31]

> I have already intimated that I did not myself believe in the charges
> against [the vicar] and I am absolutely certain that no person would
> be so foolish as to believe those charges, supported as they are only
> by the word of a blackmailer, [and] in passing sentence . . . Mr
> Justice Finlay said he did not for one moment accept [the defend-
> ant's] view that there was foundation for the threats he used, from
> the moral point of view it was not easy to say whether his conduct
> was more contemptible if there was or was not such foundation. In
> either view what he did was almost incredibly base. Blackmail was
> always a terrible crime, and that case was a very grave example of it.

Case XIII (restitutive blackmail) Ideally the restitutive blackmailer is
not acting for himself: because the heart of blackmail in law is personal
gain translated as theft, a defendant who can show that he was setting
out to right a wrong, even though it may be a personal wrong, can
sometimes attract the sympathy of the court. The following is an
example:

At West Ham police court on the 27th April 1891, a solicitor's
clerk was committed for trial at the Old Bailey. The charge was one
of sending a threatening letter with intent to extort money from his
former employer who had discharged him 'for being inattentive'.
Distressed at the thought of losing his job, the defendant asked a
fellow employee to intercede on his behalf and as a consequence the
notice was withdrawn. Some time after he found a new job and
moved on.

On 22 April 1891 his former employer received a signed letter which, in the words of 'The Times' report,

> made an assertion in respect of the prosecutor and asked for an
> apology and the payment of £25 towards the West Ham Hospital.
> The prisoner said the letter was true and he had consulted a
> solicitor having written the letter on his instructions. It was
> stated the prisoner afterwards said there was no truth in the
> letter and that he did not want any of the money.

The defence advanced the argument that the relevant legislation
'contemplated a person seeking to put money into his own pocket'.
It was submitted that the prisoner had not sought to do this and the
money he had asked for was for payment to a hospital. Witnesses were
then called to speak of the good character of the accused. Finding
him not guilty the foreman of the jury said: 'The jury wish me to add
this — that we believe he had just cause.'[32]

Other blackmailers who apparently believed they had just cause have
not been treated so considerately. In our society rules governing the
transference of wealth and property from one individual or group to
another are such that claims of social justice are often as much honoured
in the breach as in the observance; what may seem like social justice to
one man may well represent a flagrant breach of the rules of the well-
ordered life to another. When a comfortably situated man received a
letter signed 'Justice' demanding £15 to be sent to Whitechapel post
office, he took it straight to the police who afterwards arrested the
writer. He turned out to be a fifty-seven year-old down-and-out, said
to have been living in workhouses and casual wards for years. When
arrested he was quoted as saying: 'Yes I wrote it. What can I do? You
see I am down and out and I would rather be in prison than in the
casual wards of the workhouses. It was either starvation or a lunatic
asylum or getting money somehow. The strain of living as I have done
is terrible both mentally and physically.'

The police said there were three previous convictions against the
prisoner in England and two in Canada. The prisoner, they thought
seemed to want to get into prison, he had called Scotland Yard on
one occasion and asked to be locked up. He said he had written a
letter to a newspaper editor and another to a second 'gentleman'
demanding money. He knew nothing against the complainant to
whom he had written 'Unless I receive this [the £15] by Tuesday
next certain information in my possession will be made use of to put
you in the dock. The Recorder told the defendant that he wanted to
be kept at public expense and he would only cater for him because
he was a danger to society. His only cause for regret, he added, was

that he could not give the 'cat'. The only way to stop blackmail was through the 'cat'.[33]

Compensatory blackmail is quite a different matter from restitutive or vengeful blackmail. The emphasis is upon cash payment for personal injury in the past, on the basis of the same set of social assumptions supporting libel actions. Cash is seen as actuarily related to disturbing incidents in the blackmailer's life. Compensatory blackmail resembles relational entitlement in that the blackmailer asks for cash from someone with whom he has had a prior relationship. The difference being that a compensatory blackmailer asks for payment following a break in the relationship, in lieu of benefits to be expected in the future, or to counterbalance losses in the past.

Case XIV (compensatory blackmail) Unsuccessful litigants sometimes feel they are entitled to compensation for financial losses sustained in a civil action. A publican, previously subject to a civil action by the brewery whose tenant he had been, was charged with demanding £1,918 with menaces from the solicitor who had acted for the company concerned. It seems that the affair had found its way into Chancery and in view of the expenses of litigation the accused was made bankrupt. He then began writing abusive letters to the solicitor blaming him for the loss. In court the defendant read out a long statement in which he said he wrote the letters to make the victim prosecute him. He wanted to make his position public and had no intention of hurting the complainant.[34]

(3) Personally pressurising situations

Uniting compensatory, restitutive, and vengeful blackmail, is a conventional ideology of social justice which certain blackmailers are able to incorporate into their actual demands for money, or use them after discovery, as the most appropriate means of explaining to their inquisitors the course of events. The distinction between the various vocabularies employed is at all times one of emphasis. Inevitably cases occur combining facets of all these themes. The general point is that blackmailers are above all selective — primarily *in terms of their every-day social relations* with those who become defined as victims. Second-hand insight into the processes making for the selectivity of their actions can be gleaned by taking into account the social assumptions permeating various justificatory statements put forward over time. Whilst the content of such accounts varies the form remains intact.

The category 'personally pressurising situations' denotes two forms of justification we can epitomise as 'cruel necessity'. In both moral crusade, and blackmail under threat, the offender indicates he is regretfully compelled to initiate the transaction, either from a pose of self-righteous superior morality, or because he himself is under some sort of threat.

A moral crusade for the blackmailer is a very limited affair.[35] With the exception of the Chrimes case, large numbers of victims are never involved in any of the blackmail cases coming before the courts, although, a certain group of people may be singled out for attention by the blackmailer. It may be thought that this type of justification should be subsumed under social justice but it does seem important to separate it out since we are specifically referring to these cases where a blackmailer is brought, often by chance, into contact with certain individuals against whom it is possible (and even considered socially desirable), to make accusations of deviant behaviour. Such encounters differ from entrepreneurial blackmail in that the offender has not manipulated the victim into a vulnerable position in order to generate discreditable information. Personal pressure can be translated into pained surprise — the blackmailer suddenly discovers it is his 'unfortunate duty' to transmit information unless he is dissuaded through some payment; in addition, a punitive element may accompany this muted expression of moral outrage.

Commercialised voyeurism represents quite a popular variation on the theme of chance moral victimisation. Not long ago, two young men received a six months' suspended sentence for threatening a woman with the circulation of intimate coloured photographs recording her adultery. The had asked for £100 and when trapped by the police with a fake package, admitted they had no photographs but needed the money.

Some time in the summer of 1899 a young man and his girl friend were 'seated on a rail adjoining a public path, in a field . . . [when] . . . the prisoner made his appearance, accused the couple of behaving improperly and said he had witnesses as to what occurred, and he would "have to be squared". When the case reached the police court the accused pleaded, as a defendant of public morals, that he had simply called on the prosecutor to account for his indecent conduct. Under cross-examination the young victim denied putting his girl friend's waterproof over his knees. He did put it over his shoulders and button it up and he did it for fun, but his motives and actions were beyond reproach.

In response to the magistrate's observation that the prisoner had no right to demand money even if the complainant was acting indecently, defence counsel stated: 'My witnesses will deny any threats were used'. These denials came to nothing, the defendant was committed for trial at the Old Bailey.[36]

Case XV (moral crusade)   At Lincoln Assizes in 1925, a seventeen-year-old railway clerk pleaded guilty to writing a letter purporting to come from the 'Crimson Triangle League' demanding £50. The letter alleged the recipient, a married man, had behaved 'as a rotter' towards a girl to whom the young man in question was engaged. The 'Crimson Triangle League', it was stated, had thoughtfully informed the young man of this conduct. Proceedings against the victim would be stopped if he paid the money.

Acting under police advice the victim replied in the pre-addressed envelope provided, asking for a meeting. Responding, the defendant wrote that the girl had been ordered fresh air and that £50 was required to buy a motorcycle to take her for rides. It must be settled within a month, he added, as he had to report to the 'League'. When arrested the young man had the victim's reply and a copy of the League letter in his pocket. He admitted he had written the letters to frighten the victim, following allegations against him by his fiancée.

Given an excellent character, the accused was allowed bail throughout the trial. Defence counsel described the letters as the height of a fantastic imagination. There was no truth in the allegations against the victim and the defendant was highly spoken of by his employer. Every effort would be made to see his future was not jeopardised by this incident. The judge remarked that this was one of the worst offences known to the law but after what had been said he would not send the accused to prison; he would 'give him a chance to recover his character'. Britain's only representative of the 'Crimson Triangle League' was thus bound over on a personal surety of £10, and two other sureties of £10 for two years.[37]

Blackmail under threat occurs when the detected blackmailer blames others for forcing him to write blackmailing letters or make verbal demands. Cases have been reported where offenders have blamed threatening gang members for their actions. An incident occurred in 1897, for example, where a man in charge of one of the refreshment bars in London's Victoria Park, who was said to have a good character, affirmed he 'was told by a number of toughs' to write the incriminating letter, to which Mr Justice Darling replied that 'he hoped the County Council would see that Victoria Park was kept more respectably than in the past', and the defendant received twelve months' imprisonment with hard labour.[38]

To some extent blackmail under threat is marginal to our whole consideration of justifications for blackmail. Referring back to Scott and Lyman's distinction between justifications and excuses, as types of accounts, blackmail under threat smacks too much of an excuse, although it would be risky to draw any hard and fast line. Also not considered strictly relevant, are those statements by blackmailers or defence counsel emphasising the involuntary nature of the action — alternatively a manifestation of mental disturbance, the influence of alcohol, shell shock, the affects of sensational literature, and other factors. As it turns out there have been few of these, the majority of recorded statements advocating relations of exchange and varying conceptions of social justice.

Allowing for the possibility the defendant *may believe* he is entitled to demand or negotiate some return, considerably complicates the issue but certainly helps us to appreciate why the oversimplified stereotype of blackmail has proved so popular. It carries 'a freight of truth'. The law now expressly recognises conscious criminal intent as a significant variable for distinguishing blackmailers from non-blackmailers. If anything this will have the effect of reinforcing the stereotype.

In closing, let us compare what has gone before with one man's justification of systematic blackmail:[39]

One of the men in the hostel is Stanley B, whom I came across a long time ago, before the war, in Parkhurst where he was doing a very long sentence for blackmail. He's still at it, or at least he was up to the time he got his P.D. sentence (preventive detention). He's always concentrated on what he calls 'the homosexual trade', getting men into compromising situations with a number of good-looking youths he had on his payroll, and then posing as their irate father or guardian and demanding money to send the boy away, at great expense, 'to start a new life'.
He said a Scotland Yard Detective had published his memoirs and devoted nearly the whole of one instalment to Stanley under the heading'One Man I Would Never Shake Hands With'. Stanley says it's the only thing he can find any enthusiasm for. He said the idea put about by judges and the Press that victims lived in fear and trembling of the blackmailer's next demand was nonsense. 'Some of my clients', he said aggressively, 'look upon me almost as a friend, because I know more about them often than even their own wives do!'

Even the entrepreneurial blackmailer can define himself as providing a personal service via the commercialisation of the confessional.

The traditional notion, exemplified in most of the existing literature, that the blackmailer is someone who has taken an *undue* advantage of the victim, derives from our fear of the potentially disruptive consequences attending detected cases, and ignores the contribution of concealed blackmail to social order. Blackmailers, as we have seen, are at best attributed a situationally delimited sense of power and at worst, an organising lust for power: Raymond Chandler — the doyen of crime novelists — allows his private detective, Philip Marlowe, to reflect our sense of outrage, 'people like Louis Vannier do not commit suicide. A blackmailer, even a scared blackmailer, has a sense of power and loves it'.[40] However, if we follow the Theft Act and allow that many of those accused of blackmail may not see themselves as blackmailers at all, then not only are we working towards a deeper understanding of reputational blackmail, but we are also beginning to realise that blackmailers are not necessarily much different from the rest of us in their approach to selected interpersonal relations.

Notes

Introduction

1 The barrister, C.E. Bechhofer Roberts, in his foreword to the transcript of a cause célèbre of the 1920s, 'The Mr A Case', London, Jarrolds, 1950.
2 Erving Goffman, who sees individual reputation as the product of skilful information management, has labelled this form of blackmail, 'full' or 'classic' blackmail. 'Stigma: Notes on the Management of Spoiled Identity', Harmondsworth, Penguin, 1971.
3 A. Bodelsen, 'Hit and Run, Run, Run,' Harmondsworth, Penguin, 1971.
4 P. Loraine, 'Photographs Have Been Sent To Your Wife', London, Fontana, 1971.
5 See Henry Cecil's description of the contents of blackmailing letters received by the victim in his novel, 'The Asking Price', London, Sphere, 1968.
6 V. Canning, 'The Scorpio Letters', London, Pan, 1966.
7 T. Lewis, 'Plender', London, Pan, 1973.
8 Harry Ball and Lawrence Friedman have neatly summarised the overall implications of the criminal law of blackmail: 'You are not allowed to make a person buy his reputation ('blackmail'). The criminality of blackmail represents a social judgment that one may not manipulate as an income producing asset knowledge about another person's past; you may not sell to that person forbearance to use your knowledge of his guilt'. H.V. Ball and L.M. Friedman, The use of criminal sanctions in the enforcement of economic legislation:

a sociological view, 'Stanford Law Review', vol. 17, 1965.

9 Bechhofer Roberts, op.cit.

10 B. Tozer, 'Confidence Crooks and Blackmailers: Their Ways and Methods', London, T. Werner Laurie, 1929.

11 J.C. Ellis, 'Blackmailers & Co', London, Selwyn & Blount, 1928.

12 Fleeting references to blackmail frequently appear in studies of sexual deviation. With certain exceptions, to be quoted later, these studies rarely describe blackmail in any detail, concentrating for the most part upon the deviation (homosexuality, adultery, promiscuity, etc.) as such. For one impressionistic account of the interrelationship between blackmail and white slavery, see S. Barlay, 'Sex Slavery: A Documentary Report on The International Scene Today', London, Heinemann, 1968.

Chapter 1 The Concept of Blackmail

1 L. Humphreys, 'Out of The Closets', Englewood Cliffs, Prentice-Hall, 1972.

2 The concept of 'criminalisation' is often used by sociologists of deviance to refer to what Edwin Schur has called 'the perils of over-legislating', meaning that various activities (e.g. abortion, homosexuality, the misuse of drugs), are transformed into criminal offences in a context where large sectors of the population find these services particularly relevant to the maintenance of their way of life. Legislating against such pursuits does not effectively control them; it may merely help to drive them underground. E.M. Schur, 'Our Criminal Society: The Social and Legal Sources of Crime in America', Englewood Cliffs, Prentice-Hall, 1969. With regard to blackmail, the criminal law can hardly be said to have hustled the offence into obscurity. Recognition of the existence of blackmail in the wider community brought greater publicity and, arguably, taught would-be blackmailers the need for greater subtlety when attempting to gain their ends. Equally, blackmail differs from abortion, homosexuality, drug taking and the like, in so far as it is subject to massive disapproval throughout all levels of society.

3 G.T. Crook (ed.), 'The Complete Newgate Calendar', vol. 4, London, Navarre Society, 1926.

4 Writers generally agree the word 'blackmail' made its first literary appearance in Sir Walter Scott's 'Waverley'. 1814. Waverley, a stranger to Scotland, hears the word spoken and discovers its connection with the border country. Blackmail, he is told, is protection money paid to chiefs to guarantee freedom from

physical attack by themselves, other chieftains, or robbers. D. Spearman, 'The Novel and Society', London, Routledge & Kegan Paul, 1966.

5 J. Bellamy, 'Crime and Public Order in England in The Later Middle Ages', London, Routledge & Kegan Paul, 1973.

6 Ibid.

7 E.J. Hobsbawm has asserted that social banditry differs radically from other types of criminality. Social bandits are a special kind of 'peasant outlaw whom the lord and state regard as criminals, but who remain within peasant society, and are considered by their people as heroes, as champions, avengers, fighters for justice, perhaps even leaders of liberation, and any case as men to be admired, helped and supported'. 'Bandits', London, Weidenfeld & Nicolson, 1969. On outlaws generally, see M.McIntosh, Changes in the organisation of thieving, in S. Cohen (ed.), 'Images of Deviance', Harmondsworth, Penguin, 1971. Blackmailing in all its forms may, of course, be attributed to both bandits and outlaws, whatever their political persuasion.

8 E. Griew, 'The Theft Act', London, Sweet & Maxwell, 1968.

9 'The Times', 19, 24 December 1885.

10 'The Times', 12 December 1898.

11 'The Times', 23 November 1885.

12 F. Hill, 'Crime: Its Amount, Causes and Remedies', London, John Murray, 1853.

13 Quoted in L. Radzinowicz, 'A History of English Criminal Law and Its Administration From 1750', vol. 1, London, Stevens, 1948.

14 Ibid. Notorious, because it considerably extended the range of offences carrying the death penalty.

15 Ibid.

16 Ibid.

17 A.H. Campbell, The anomalies of blackmail, 'Law Quarterly Review', vol. LX, 1939.

18 W.H.D. Winder, The development of blackmail, 'Modern Law Review', vol. V, 1941.

19 'F. v. Knewland', 1796, 2 Leach 721.

20 Winder, op. cit.

21 'R. v. Hickman', 1784, 1 Leach 278

22 Quoted by H. Montgomery Hyde, A look at the law, in M. Rubinstein (ed.), 'Wicked, Wicked Libels', London, Routledge & Kegan Paul, 197?

23 S.F. Harris, 'Principles of The Criminal Law', London, Stevens & Haynes, 1904.

24 J. Dean, 'Hatred, Ridicule or Contempt: A Book of Libel Cases', Harmondsworth, Penguin, 1964.

25 Winder, op. cit., stresses that because 'so few cases on the subject

business and pleasure and public and private experience.

(2)   Those who are vulnerable to blackmail at certain stages in their life careers, or who may be subject to what Goode calls 'individual fluctuations in personal integration'.[35] Specific private or public acts render such people sensitive about their public image with reference to their status at particular points in time, rather than because they occupy a continuously vulnerable position.

(3)   Those whose sense of worth is heavily dependent on their relations with others who have some influence over them. Since many of us are in this position a distinction must be made in terms of *perceived advantage.* If a person believes himself to be vulnerable then this will affect his bargaining power in encounters with the blackmailer just as much as the perceptions of the latter can lead him to overreach his hand and end up before the courts. This final group includes all those interactions at the 'everyday' level of living, productive of the commonplace offence of blackmail.

A sense of respectable public reputation secured against the 'breath of scandal' is consequently more than a meal ticket: in the competitive, hierarchical world it retains its persistent symbolic value as mediator between the observed approval of others, attributing some degree of competence or success, and the personal experience of self-esteem.[36]

Four types of blackmail

Descriptions of criminal blackmail often blur the critical distinction between attempted and completed blackmail.[37] Three years following the close of the Second World War a postman pleaded guilty to opening a packet during the course of transmission and demanding £5 with menaces. It was stated by the prosecution that the victim had a parcel sent to her from California containing a letter and a brassière. The man who had so rashly opened the parcel discovered the letter accompanying this intimate article was couched in endearing terms. He phoned the victim, conveyed his interpretation of the materials described, and the possible interest of the victim's husband, and was subsequently arrested, the victim pretending to go along with his demands, so the completion of the transaction could be observed by a hidden policeman.

We can make a useful sociological distinction between attempted and completed blackmail in terms of exploratory negotiation. Exploratory negotiations involve a variety of interchanges between the persons concerned; during these interchanges, the nature of the transaction may change as some sort of relationship is established between the

are reported', it is difficult to ascertain the legal sources of prosecutions against nineteenth-century blackmailers, who did not threaten actual physical violence.

26 Giving judgment following the conviction of the ex-employer of a stock and share broker, at Liverpool Assizes. The prisoner pleaded guilty to sending a letter demanding money with menaces. After leaving his employer's services, he wrote personally and through a solicitor, allegedly demanding money due to him for wages and expenses. The letter from the solicitor read in part, 'My client also claims compensation from you. Unless I receive a satisfactory communication from you by the time named such steps will be taken as my client may be advised to adopt'. After sentencing the offender to five years penal servitude, Mr Justice Wills observed that the letter written by the solicitor, who was not charged at the time with any offence, was scarcely less criminal in character, and he intended to pass it on to the authorities for further consideration. 'The Times', 19 November, 1885.

27 C. Mercier, 'Crime and Criminals', University of London Press, 1918. Mercier, who was a doctor, noted that reputational blackmail was becoming 'far from infrequent' as extortion by time-honoured physical violence declined. 'No doubt', he wrote, 'it would be difficult in many cases to prove intention and other ingredients in crime. Nevertheless they are proved, and criminals are punished for them'.

28 B. Hogan, Blackmail: another view, 'Criminal Law Review', 1966.

29 Larceny Act, 1916, (6+76. 5C. 50). The three relevant sections are: 'S.29. (1) Every person who — (i) utters, knowing the contents thereof, any letter or writing demanding of any person with menaces, and without any reasonable or probable cause, any property or valuable thing; (ii) utters, knowing the contents thereof, any letter or writing accusing or threatening to accuse any other person (whether living or dead) of any such crime; shall be guilty of felony, and on conviction thereof liable to penal servitude for life, and, if a male under the age of sixteen years, to be once privately whipped in addition to any other punishment to which he may by law be liable.

(2)   Every person who with intent to defraud or injure any other person — (a) by any unlawful violence to or restraint of the person of another, or (b) by accusing or threatening to accuse any person (whether living or dead) of any such crime or of any felony, compels or induces any person to execute, make, accept, endorse, alter, or destroy the whole or any part of any valuable security, or to write, impress, or affix the name of any person, company, firm or co-partnership, or the seal of any body corporate, company or society upon or to any paper or parchment in order that it may be

afterwards made or converted into or used or dealt with as a valuable security, shall be guilty of felony and on conviction thereof liable to penal servitude for life.

(3)   This section applies to any crime punishable with death, or penal servitude for not less than seven years, or to any assault with intent to commit any rape, or any attempt to commit any rape, or any solicitation, persuasion, promise, or threat offered or made to any person, whereby to move or induce any person to commit or permit the abominable crime of buggery, either with mankind or with any animal.

(4)   For the purposes of this Act it is immaterial whether any menaces or threats be of violence, injury, or accusation to be caused or made by the offender or by any other person.

S.30. Every person who with menaces or by force demands of any person anything capable of being stolen with intent to steal the same shall be guilty of felony and on conviction thereof liable to penal servitude for any term not exceeding five years.

S.31. Every person who with intent — (a) to extort any valuable thing from any person, or (b) to induce any person to confer or procure for any person any appointment or office of profit or trust.

(1)   publishes or threatens to publish any libel upon any other person (whether living or dead); or

(2)   directly or indirectly threatens to print or publish, or directly or indirectly proposes to abstain from or offers to prevent the printing or publishing of any matter or thing touching any other person (whether living or dead);

shall be guilty of a misdemeanour and on conviction thereof liable to imprisonment with or without hard labour, for any term not exceeding two years.

30 G.L. Williams, Blackmail, 'Criminal Law Review', 1954.
31 Criminal Law revision Committee, 'Eighth Report, Theft and Related Offences', London, HMSO, 1966, Cmnd 2977.
32 Ibid.
33 Griew, op. cit.
34 Ibid.
35 'House of Lords Debates, Official Report', vol. 289, 13 February — 7 March, 1968.
36 Griew, op. cit.
37 'House of Commons Debates, Official Report', vol. 763, 23 April — 3 May 1968.
38 H.T. Fitch, 'Traitors Within: The Adventures of Detective Inspector Herbert T. Fitch', London, Hurst & Blackett, 1933.
39 'The Times', 2 April 1924.
40 Blackmail, 'Police Journal', vol. IV, 1931.

41 T. Humphreys, 'A Book of Trials: Personal Recollections of An Eminent Judge of The High Court', London, Pan, 1955. Unfortunately, the author fails to describe the blackmail cases in which he appeared, perhaps because they were, for the most part, undramatic affairs.

42 Most statistically oriented criminology texts ignore it completely; presumably, the figures are considered insignificant.

43 H. Mannheim, 'Social Aspects of Crime in England Between the Wars', London, Allen & Unwin, 1940.

44 'Criminal Statistics (England and Wales) 1955', London, HMSO, 1956. A paragraph explained the reduction of the twofold system to a single category: the previous classification of offences was 'a little misleading and it has been decided that they can more satisfactorily be grouped together under the title "Blackmail" '. Obviously, this means the Criminal Statistics now give us no indication of the kinds of activities prosecuted under the most recent blackmail legislation, though the category has been expanded to meet the broader conceptualisation of criminal 'menace'.

45 S.T. Felstead (edited by Lady Muir), 'Sir Richard Muir: A Memoir of a Public Prosecutor', London, John Lane the Bodley Head, 1927.

46 It is frequently observed that blackmail is responsible for many suicides, yet the extensive literature on suicide offers little corroborative evidence. I have discovered several instances where blackmail is cited as the cause of attempted or completed suicide, but very few conclusive cases. Theoretical connections between blackmail and suicide tend be most prominent in discussions of unreported crime, and its implications for the 'dark figure' of undetected criminal offences, occurring continuously around us. See, for example, S. Schafer, 'The Victim and His Criminal: A Study in Functional Responsibility', New York, Random House, 1968.

47 Stamping out blackmail, 'The Times', 24 February 1930.

48 M.L. Macnaghten, 'Days of My Years', London, Edward Arnold, 1914.

49 J.K. Ferrier (formerly Detective-Inspector, Scotland Yard), 'Crooks and Crime: Describing The Methods of Criminals From The Area Sneak to The Professional Card Sharper, Forger or Murderer and The Various Ways in which They are Circumvented and Captured,' London, Seeley, Service, 1928.

50 At the trial of a woman who pleaded guilty to sending a letter demanding £20, accusing a master tailor of a crime. The prosecutor's name and address were not disclosed. The suppression of blackmail, 'The Times', 20 September 1933.

51 J.C. Turner, 'Kenny's Outline of Criminal Law', Cambridge University Press, 1952.

52 'The Times', 15 June 1921.

53 'The Times', 26 July 1932.

54 The doctor had received a letter threatening to accuse him of 'the crime of abortion' unless he made a loan of £300 to the writer, with whom he was completely unacquainted. 'The Times', 11 November 1936.

Chapter 2 'True Blackmail'

1 J.K. Ferrier, 'Crooks and Crime: Describing the Methods of Criminals from the Area Sneak to the Professional Card Sharper, Forger or Murderer, and The Various Ways in which They are Circumvented and Captured', London, Seeley, Service, 1928.

2 Blackmail, 'The New York Times', 23 September 1874.

3 Ibid.

4 'The Times', 13 November 1897. She was sentenced to eighteen months' imprisonment with hard labour. Prosecuting counsel stated that after her arrest extensive enquiries had been made into her background. It appeared she had acted in collusion with her husband and had attempted blackmail before. She was removed from the court proclaiming herself the victim of a police plot.

5 Ironically, it was the speculator, Horatio Bottomley, who established the widely circulating magazine 'John Bull', prior to his eventual conviction for financial malpractice. Not a few blackmailers have threatened to send their information to this publication.

6 'The Times', 15 January, 11 February, 12 February 1897.

7 'The Times', 22, 23 November 1899.

8 'The Times' 19 March 1912.

9 J.C. Ellis, 'Blackmailers & Co.', London, Selwyn & Blount, 1928.

10 B. Tozer, 'Confidence Crooks and Blackmailers: Their Ways and Methods', London. T. Werner Laurie, 1929.

11 H. Pearson, 'Labby: The Life of Henry Labouchère', London, Hamish Hamilton, 1936. Over in the USA, Labouchère's venture, originating in a passionate sense of social justice, was allegedly the inspiration of a more dubious interpretation of the notion of the 'public interest' by Colonel William D'Alton Mann, from 1891 to 1920 the proprietor of a notorious and widely read essay in scandal-mongering journalism called 'Town Topics, The Journal of Society'. Published in New York, D'Alton Mann's lucrative manipulation of society gossip was a prominent feature

of American 'high life'. Although D'Alton Mann managed to avoid
criminal conviction, it was alleged in a sensational court case, that
he derived a considerable income from promises to refrain from
publishing biographical details detrimental to a host of members of
the wealthy entrepreneurial classes, who wished to present
themselves as fit and proper associates of the respectable social
élite. Throughout his career, D'Alton Mann insisted his occupation
was not blackmail, but 'the elevation of society'. A full account of
D'Alton Mann's flamboyant professional life appears in A, Logan,
'The Man Who Robbed The Robber Barons', London, Gollancz,
1966.

12 Ibid.

13 J. Symonds and K. Grant (eds), 'The Confessions of Aleister Crowley',
London, Jonathan Cape, 1969.

14 A not uncommon assumption today.

15 F.J. Higginbottom, 'The Vivid Life: A Journalist's Career', London,
Simpkin Marshall, 1934.

16 Tozer, op. cit.

17 K. Thomas, The double standard, 'Journal of The History of Ideas',
vol. 20, 1959. Thomas explores the history of the traditional
'English insistence on female chastity' (compared with a more indulgent
attitude towards clandestine male promiscuity), and relates this to
legislation affecting marital life which embodies 'the view that men
have property in women and that the value of this property is
immeasurably diminished if the woman at any time has sexual
relations with anyone other than her husband'.

18 The word 'permissive' is used here to signify 'giving permission for',
or tolerating certain activities. 'Permissive' should not be exclusively
interpreted as sexual licence, as some critics of the so-called
'permissive society' would have us believe. In so far as ordered
social conduct comprises a framework of observable controls, every
society is a permissive society.

19 F. Oughton, 'Ten Guineas A Day: A Portrait of The Private Detective',
London, John Long, 1961. Oughton notes that had it not been for
the Matrimonial Causes Act 1857, 'which was responsible for the
formation of the divorce court as we know it, we would never have
had the many hundreds of private detectives and agencies that now
make a profession out of matrimonial investigation'. The Act had
repercussions for the organisation of protective and investigative
skills: 'But for the 1857 Act we would still have security, not
detection, agencies, small organisations for looking after houses,
factories, offices and other vulnerable premises. The very terms,
'private detective' and 'private investigator' would never have come
into use.'

20 Quoted in C. Pearl, 'The Girl With The Swansdown Seat', New York, Signet Books, 1958.

21 F. Harris, 'My Life and Loves', London, Corgie Books, 1966. Harris was a notoriously egocentric and unreliable writer but press coverage of the Campbell case was considerable. H. Wyndham, 'The Mayfair Calendar: Some Society Causes Célèbres', London, Hutchinso 1925, notes 'The Times' declined to print some of the evidence out of deference to the susceptibilities of its readers. 'Other journals . . . were less particular, and served up a very full report of the unhappy conditions under which the parties to the action had lived'.

22 'The Times', 14 December 1886.

23 Ibid.

24 J. Johnson (ed.), 'An Orator of Justice: A Speech Biography of Viscount Buckmaster', London, Ivor Nicholson & Watson, 1932.

25 'The Times', 5 December 1898.

26 Gossip columnists represent this development. Walter Winchell, the famous American columnist of the 1930s and 40s, has been described as the inventor of 'keyhole journalism': the man who 'abolished privacy for ever'. J. Crosby, Walter Winchell was the true father of gutter journalism, 'Observer' 27 February 1972.

27 H. Herd, 'The March of Journalism: The History of The British Press From 1622 to The Present Day', London, Allen & Unwin, 1952.

28 Changes in journalism occurred throughout the western world. In Britain, the Harmsworths of Fleet Street pushed the trend prosperously along. Their brand of popular journalism helped to shape public taste, and although overtly wedded to middle-class notions of the respectable hearth and home, thrived upon the publication of sensational criminal and other 'human interest' stories. In passing it is worth noting Alfred Harmsworth's distaste for 'penny dreadfuls', those colourful novelettes which were sometimes described as the stimulus behind certain youthful attempts at blackmail. See P. Ferris, 'The House of Northcliffe: The Harmsworths of Fleet Street', London, Weidenfeld & Nicolson, 1971.

29 With reference to company, as distinct from criminal law, Rita Christie has written: 'A general view of the effect of economic changes upon business organisation in the nineteenth century pinpoints the main areas within which modern company law developed. On the one hand, there were the structural changes leading to the emergence of the limited liability joint stock company as a major feature and vehicle of economic development; on the other hand, the subsequent evolution of a set of relationships between the investor and the company with whom his capital was

placed. The growing body of modern company law concerned itself with the technical aspects of the former, and, as the abuses following upon the divorce of the ownership from the control of capital became apparent, the responsibilities of the managing body and the safeguarding of the owner's property, largely by the device of increased publicity.' R.M. Christie, The legality of business, University of London, Unpublished M. Phil. thesis, 1969.

30 'The Times', 22 Cotober 1936.

31 A.J.P. Taylor, in his preface to Frances Stevenson's recollections of her life with Lloyd George, observes the relations 'between Lloyd George and Frances Stevenson were a secret, respected even by his bitterest opponents, during his life and for some years afterwards. Now there is no reason for concealment'. A.J.P. Taylor (ed.), 'Lloyd George: A Diary By Frances Stevenson', London, Hutchinson, 1971.

32 Laud Humphreys, one of the most skilled recorders of secretive impersonal relations, remarked in his study of 'instant sex' in male toilets, 'Because I was unable to observe any blackmail in progress, I rely upon the accounts of respondents for data on instances of extortion and payoffs to the police'. 'Tearoom Trade: A Study of Homosexual Encounters in Public Places', London, Duckworth, 1970.

33 'The Times', 31 March 1938.

34 Ellis, op. cit., Introduction.

35 My interviews with certain provincial C.I.D. officers, showed the largest number of offences investigated involved some form of physical threat. Distinguishing the more robust forms of blackmail from the reputational variety (resulting, I was told, from the influx of 'effete' individuals into the larger urban areas), one informant asserted that the incidence of all types of extortion had remained static throughout this century. Nevertheless, he thought, there was evidence of extensive 'moral blackmail' in the community. In this particular case, crime figures for the locality revealed no significant variation from the 1930s to the present day in the minuscule number of offences known to the police. Figures I have seen for other areas, outside London, to not offer an alternative picture.

36 For a discussion of the functional significance of stereotypes for an understanding of the 'crime problem' generally, see D. Chapman, 'Sociology and The Stereotype of The Criminal, London, Tavistock, 1968. Chapman argues that those we learn to call 'criminals' are selected by the social system to serve as scapegoats. Known offenders are, therefore, unrepresentative of the true extent of dishonest behaviour in a society where there is 'much ambivalence and confusion about morals', and where the symbolically enforced moral order

frequently conflicts with actual social practice.

37 Walter Lippman defined the stereotype as a 'picture in our heads', to which we must relate experience. 'Public Opinion', New York, Harcourt Brace, 1922.

38 Logan, op. cit.

39 The clause, introduced by Henry Labouchère, made male homosexual acts of 'gross indecency', whether in public or in private, punishable with a maximum sentence of two years' imprisonment with hard labour. This repressive legislation — criminalising homosexuality and thus widening the prospects of blackmail — was not repealed until The Sexual Offences Act 1967, which followed certain of the more liberal recommendations of the Wolfenden Committee's 'Report of The Committee on Homosexual Offences and Prostitution', London, HMSO, 1957, Cmnd 247. For a useful history of the clause and its effect on the public treatment of some men detected in homosexual acts, see H. Montgomery Hyde, 'The Other Love: A Historical and Contemporary Survey of Homosexuality in Britain', London, Heinemann, 1970.

40 H. Montgomery Hyde, 'Famous Trials: Oscar Wilde', Harmondsworth, Penguin, 1962, provides a detailed exposition of Wilde's trials.

41 R. Roberts, 'The Classic Slum: Salford Life in The First Quarter of The Century', Manchester University Press, 1971.

42 'The Times', 8 May 1895.

43 R. Croft-Cooke, 'The Unrecorded Life of Oscar Wilde', London, W.H. Allen, 1972.

44 Ellis, op. cit.

45 'The Times', 14 February 1931. B was sentenced to eighteen months imprisonment with hard labour.

46 'The Times', 20, 21 January, 19 February 1931.

47 'The Times', 10 February, 1936.

48 Alleged blackmail, 'The Times', 3 November 1911.

49 Sir Chartres Biron, 'Without Prejudice: Impressions of Life and Law', London, Faber and Faber, 1936.

50 Pests of society, youths attempted blackmail, 'The Times', 18 November 1921.

51 See R. Fabian, 'The Anatomy of Crime', London, Pelham Books, 1970.

52 Anon., Blackmail, 'Justice of The Peace and Local Government Review', vol. CXXVI, 1962.

53 'The Times', 12 February 1938.

54 'The King v. Bernhard', Kings Bench Division-Court of Appeal 7, 22 March 1938.

55 Ibid.

56 Tozer, op. cit.

57 Stereotyped conceptions of deviants 'often contain some freight of
   truth. But they lead to distorted appraisals because they over-
   estimate within-group similarity and between-group differences, and
   they tend to be unresponsive to objective evidence.' J.L. Simmons,
   Public stereotypes of deviants, 'Social Problems', vol. 13, 1965.

Chapter 3 The Master Blackmailer

1 Quoted in D.N. Pritt, 'Spies and Informers in The Witness Box',
   London, Bernard Harrison, 1958.
2 Sir Arthur Conan Doyle, Charles Augustus Milverton in, 'The Return
   of Sherlock Holmes', London, Pan, 1954.
3 'The Times', 6, 11, 21 June 1892.
4 The case of attempted blackmail is taken from 'The Times'. The
   blackmailing letters are reproduced from W. Teignmouth Shore's
   edited version of Cream's trial for the murder of Matilda Clover,
   which began at the Old Bailey on 17 October 1892, 'The Trial of
   Thomas Neill Cream', London and Edinburgh, William Hodge, 1923.
5 Cream's counsel entered a protest over the press publicity the case
   received. The current treatment, he said, would prejudice his client
   in the eyes of the jury should he be unfortunate enough to be committed
   for trial: 'The prisoner was at present only charged with blackmailing;
   the case was sub judice, and he ventured to suggest that the press
   should be more careful and guarded with respect to what they were
   publishing about it'. The magistrate agreed with these comments; a
   newspaper report of a charge should be nothing more than that,
   anything else was unfair and improper. 'The Times', 6, 11, 21 June
   1892.
6 Teignmouth Shore, op. cit.
7 C.J. Ettinger, 'The Problem of Crime', London, Ray Long & Richard
   Smith, 1932.
8 'Badger game' : a slang term for 'using an amorous man's indiscretion
   as grounds for blackmail'. E. Partridge, 'A Dictionary of The
   Underworld', London, Routledge & Kegan Paul, 1950.
9 C.E. Bechhofer Roberts, 'The Mr A Case', London, Jarrolds,
   1950.
10 A.M. Sullivan, 'The Last Sergeant: The Memoirs of Sergeant A.M.
   Sullivan, Q.C.', London, Macdonald, 1952.
11 The woman in the case — a housewife — had been threatened by a
   male acquaintance with the revelation of an abortion, he was under
   the impression she and her sister had performed at home. In fact
   he had obtained this erroneous information from a servant who had

totally misinterpreted certain medical incidents. 'The Times', 6 November 1896.

12 J.C. Ellis, 'Blackmailers & Co.', London, Selwyn & Blount. 1928.

13 H. Rossetti Angeli, 'Pre-Raphaelite Twilight: The Story of Charles Augustus Howell', London, The Richards Press, 1954.

14 Quoted in C.H. Fleming, 'That Ne'er Shall Meet Again: Rossetti, Millais, Hunt', London, Michael Joseph, 1971.

15 'The Times', 23 November 1933.

16 C. Chesterton, 'Women of The Underworld', London, Stanley Paul, 1928.

17 'The Times', 7 July 1933.

18 'The Times', 30 November 1931.

19 'The Times', 19 June 1931.

20 Offenders before the courts may claim temporary and involuntary possession by the evil impulse to blackmail; had they been in a normal state of mind, it is implied, they would have resisted the temptation. Cf. Laurie Taylor's investigation of accounts by sex offenders, attributing their behaviour to a 'breakdown in mental functioning', the prompting of some 'inner impulse', or defective social skills. Taylor emphasises that statements offered by deviants after their offences have been detected, provide us with useful clues about *publicly accredited* motivational accounts, without necessarily giving insight into their actual state of mind when the acts were committed. The significance and interpretation of replies to motivational questions: the case of sex offenders, 'Sociology', vol. 6, 1972.

21 The author of this statement to the police, received twenty-two months in prison for demanding money with menaces from 'Dr X', by threatening to accuse him of performing abortions. 'The Times', 11 November 1936.

22 'The Times', 1 December 1932. The charge against a 'motor driver' and his mistress was one of demanding £10 from the 'daughter-in-law of a peer', on pain of threatening to tell her father she was living with an unmarried man. Sentencing the man to nine months' prison in the second division, the judge bound over the female accomplice — a lenient sentence for both, taking into account the male defendants 'extremely good character'.

23 M.O. Cameron, 'The Booster and The Snitch: Department Store Shoplifters', New York, Free Press, 1964. There are other ways in which detected blackmailers may resemble 'snitches' (amateur shoplifters): 'Because the adult pilferer does not think of himself, prior to his arrest, as a thief and can conceive of no in-group support for himself in that role, his arrest forces him to reject the role (at

least in so far as department shoplifting is concerned).' With the exception of occasional members of criminal gangs involved in blackmail, and a handful of people with previous records, most of the people coming before the courts in the case material presently under review, (whether they acted with others or as individuals) were not people who could be said to belong to a criminal subculture. Many of them, as we shall see in Chapter 5, denied criminal intent and it was often represented on their behalf that they had led hitherto blameless lives.

24 In an extremely valuable contribution to the sociology of law, Edwin M. Schur stresses that criminal trial deliberations are by no means based exclusively upon 'self-consistant, self contained, dependable systems of formal legal doctrine'. Law is 'man-made, man-interpreted, man-applied, and man-changed' and 'there is too little recognition of the fact that strictly speaking, a statement of 'the law' on any issue . . . tends to be merely a statement of what courts have done in the past or a prediction of what a particular court in a particular case might decide in the future'. The fact that the determination of criminal guilt or innocence is inevitably an interpretive rather than logico-scientific process, following certain unchangeable rules, means that setting out to find the 'facts' about a particular case and then attempting to tailor these facts to fit the appropriate version of a legal doctrine is a hazardous task indeed. Evidence placed before the courts is responsive to chance and subjectivity: 'the jurors are in no sense especially equipped to get at the 'facts', and some evidence that might actually help in the search for facts is barred, primarily because there is believed to be a danger in letting the jury hear it (for example, hearsay).' Also present is the danger of an emotional reaction by the jury to evidence concerning certain offences. E.M. Schur, Scientific method and the Criminal trial decision, 'Social Research', vol. 25, 1958.

25 John Irwin includes the category 'moral unworthiness' in his fourfold classification of alternative modes of interpreting criminal motivation. Moral unworthiness constitutes a 'personality model'. The other three alternatives open to penal practitioners are: (i) 'emotional disturbance'; (ii) 'subculture carrier'; (iii) 'phenomeno-logical model'. 'The Felon', Englewood Cliffs, Prentice-Hall, 1970.

26 T. Duster, 'The Legislation of Morality: Law, Drugs and Moral Judgement', New York, Free Press, 1970.

27 F. Pearce, Crime, corporations and the American social order, in I. & L. Taylor (eds), 'Politics and Deviancy', Harmondsworth, Penguin, 1973.

Chapter 4 The Business of Blackmail

1 'The Strange Death of Liberal England', London, Paladin, 1970.
2 A.R.L. Gardner, 'The Art of Crime', London, Philip Allen, 1931.
3 S.M. Miller, The credential society, 'Transaction', vol. 5, 1967.
  Miller describes the growing tendency to rely on paper qualifications
  as the only valid index of a person's occupational suitability. Practices
  of this kind discriminate, of course, against the poor the world over.
  At the same time there is a pay-off: 'Credentialing diminished our fear
  of having to make choices and exercise independent judgment. In an
  increasingly science-oriented economy, it is becoming difficult to
  know what is good performance — we do not even know what the
  product is, or how to measure it (how can we judge a physician's
  work when perhaps 70 per cent of his patients had nothing
  medically diagnosable in the first place?) . . . So we shift our
  concerns to the input — if the applicant has enough certificates
  demonstrating enough schooling, he has to be good.'
4 D.W. Ball, The problematics of respectability, in J.D. Douglas (ed.),
  'Deviance and Respectability: The Social Construction of Moral
  Meanings', New York and London, Basic Books, 1970.
5 Ibid.
6 Which does not mean that those who are unsuccessful in the eyes
  of the wider world necessarily cease to experience a sense of self-
  esteem. Although buttressed by the approval of others, self-esteem
  is in many respects a subjective phenomenon. 'By self-esteem we
  refer to the evaluation which the individual makes and customarily
  maintains with regard to himself: it expresses an attitude of
  approval or disapproval, and indicates the extent to which the
  individual believes himself to be capable, significant, successful,
  and worthy. In short, self-esteem is a *personal* judgment of
  worthiness that is expressed in the attitudes the individual holds
  toward himself.' S. Coopersmith, 'The Antecedents of Self-Esteem',
  San Francisco and London, W.H. Freeman, 1967.
7 'The Times', 3 July 1929.
8 'The Times', 27 November, 1 December 1894, 5 February 1895.
9 John Mortimer reviewing M. Rubinstein (ed.), 'Wicked, Wicked
  Libels', London, Routledge & Kegan Paul, 1972,
  Libels and Loot, 'Guardian', 23 March 1972.
10 H. Montgomery Hyde, 'Their Good Names: A Collection of Libel
  and Slander Cases', London, Hamish Hamilton, 1970.
11 Ibid.
12 L. Blom-Cooper, Free Speech — and Privacy, in Rubinstein,
  op. cit. 'The prime reason for this almost exclusive preference
  for the civil process is that a criminal prosecution brings little

personal satisfaction and no financial reward to the victim, whereas the civil action holds out the prospect of money being extracted from those who usually are of sufficiently substantial means to make them worthwhile pursuing through the courts.'

13 Solicitors say judge alone should award damages for libel, 'Guardian', 14 February 1972.

14 Oscar Wilde, An Ideal Husband, in G.F. Maine (ed.), 'The Works of Oscar Wilde', London and Glasgow, Collins, 1948.

15 R.C. Carson, 'Interaction Concepts of Personality', London, Allen & Unwin, 1970.

16 E. Goffman, 'The Presentation of Self in Everyday Life', London, Allen Lane the Penguin Press, 1968.

17 Cf. E.C. Hughes, Good people and dirty work, 'Social Problems', vol. X, 1962.

18 'Scandal is gossip made alive and exciting by the very fact that it threatens and conflicts with prevailing morality.' I. Wallace, 'The Nympho and Other Maniacs: Stories of Some Scandalous Women', London, Cassell, 1971.

19 At this trial the prisoner handed the recorder a written statement saying he had acted more like a fool than a criminal. He was, he claimed, a hard-working fellow. All to no avail — he was sentenced to ten years' penal servitude: 'Judges of this land have determined — and the Court of Criminal Appeal has strengthened their hands — to stamp out the crime of blackmail.' Stamping out blackmail. Sentence of ten years' penal servitude 'The Times', 15 January, 1931.

20 Quoted in R. Blythe, 'The Age of Illusion', Harmondsworth, Penguin, 1964.

21 J.A. Spender quoted in R. Sencourt, 'The Reign of Edward VIII, London, Panther, 1964.

22 Hypocrisy seen in tributes to Duke, 'Guardian', 6 June 1972.

23 Cf. J.R. Gusfield, 'Symbolic Crusade: Status Politics and The American Temperance Movement', Urbana and London, University of Illinois Press, 1963.

24 The defendant was acquitted and a discussion followed on whether an indictment for libel, to which she had pleaded justification, should be allowed. Defence counsel publicly exonerated the vicar from any desire to avoid further enquiries and prosecuting counsel thereupon agreed to offer no evidence. The judge confirmed the course agreed was a reasonable one. 'The Times', 7 May 1886.

25 T.H. White, 'The Age of Scandal: An Excursion Through a Minor Period', Harmondsworth, Penguin, 1962.

26 Ibid.

27 'The Times', 19 May 1931.

28 In the cold war theory and practice of national security, the advance

identification of 'risky people' applying for 'sensitive' government posts, has assumed paramount importance. In the USA, the 'investigation of sensitive job holders, one gathers, turns up all sorts of sexual misbehaviour, especially liaisons and illegitimate offspring. Such episodes are certainly not evidence of perversion, but rather of an abundance of normal impulses. They are deviations from convention that one segment of the community will view with indifference, another with compassion, another with indignation. If they are flaunted so as to outrage dominant opinion, any employer may decide that the misbehaving employee's usefulness to him is fatally impaired. If on the other hand they are concealed, presumably with shame, a security issue does arise: the possibility that an enemy agent who uncovers the secret will use it for blackmail.' R.S. Brown, 'Loyalty and Security: Employment Tests in The United States', New Haven, Yale University Press, 1958.

29 Referring to the relationship between blackmail and homosexuality, the Wolfenden Report observes, 'We would certainly not go as far as some of our witnesses have done and suggest that the opportunities for blackmail inherent in the present law would be sufficient ground for changing it. We have found it hard to decide whether the blackmailer's primary weapon is the threat of disclosure to the victim's relatives, employer or friends, with the attendant social consequences.' Adopting a position of uncertainty, the Committee felt that whatever the predominant cause of fear in the victim of homosexual blackmail, a change in the law prohibiting acts between consenting adult males in private, would at least take some advantage the law had previously placed in the hands of the blackmailer. Wolfenden Committee, 'Report of the Committee on Homosexual Offences and Prostitution', London, HMSO, 1957, Cmnd 247.

30 Becker has noted we cannot completely appreciate 'a person's commitments' unless we have some knowledge of the system of values predominant in the world in which he lives: 'What are the good things of life whose continued enjoyment can be staked on continuing to follow a consistent line of action?' H.S. Becker, Notes on the concept of commitment, 'American Journal of Sociology', vol. 66, 1960.

31 F.G. Bailey (ed.), 'Gifts and Poison: The Politics of Reputation', Oxford, Basil Blackwell, 1971. Bailey argues that membership of a community depends not on having a *good* reputation, 'only a reputation'. The immoral man is as much a part of the community as 'the moral (i.e. good) man, for he is being judged by the same moral standards'.

32 To the jury the judge remarked, 'any scoundrel could come up to

a man and make a threat of this nature and if the person threatened had not the courage to immediately send for the police he was ruined for life through not having the courage to send for the police when threatened'. 'The Times', 6 August 1886.

33 R. Furneaux, 'Great Issues in Private Courts', London, William Kimber, 1964.

34 Investigating an inconsistency between private drinking habits and publicly avowed teetotalism in a 'small rural community in Kansas', C.K. Warriner concluded the conspicuous non-consumption of alcohol functioned as an instrument for maintaining group solidarity and thus left people free to drink in the privacy of their own homes, with a clear conscience. So long as this private contravention did not challenge the 'official' morality of the village all was well, but increasing contact with the outside world brought changes in public attitudes towards drink among some villagers: 'Our evidence indicated that the official morality did not exist when there was a high degree of consensus and homogeneity of personal sentiments about drinking. It arose and became strong as this homogeneity in the community broke down — as more and more people began to believe that drinking was acceptable.' Warriner argued that official morality could not be understood simply in terms of the private behaviour of individuals, but as a 'type of collective phenomenon' dependent on degrees of social integration within the community. The nature and functions of official morality, 'American Journal of Sociology', vol. LXIV, 1958.

35 W.J. Goode, The protection of the inept, 'American Sociological Review', vol. 32, 1967. Goode classifies the 'inept' as those members of society who are less able to perform in a socially approved fashion. All groups are faced with the internal problem of protecting inept members, as well as protecting the group *from* the inept. In certain situations ineptitude will produce for the individual 'fluctuations in personal integration in the group'. One of the 'external factors' governing the willingness of the group to protect an inept member 'is that there will be less or more protection of ineptitude, depending on its consequences for the power or prestige of the person who heads the collectivity. For example, if the subordinate's ineptitude reduces the chief's power, the latter is unlikely to tolerate low competence.' Switching to the blackmail situation, we can add that one internal source of collective displeasure experienced by the victim may result from a failure on his part to conceal his personal indulgences from some external, potentially unsympathetic witness.

36 Laud Humphreys's researches revealed that men in 'dependent occupations', and with wives, were more restricted in their access

119

to the means of protecting themselves against discovery than men 'of greater autonomy'. Accordingly, they tended to assume 'the breast-plate of righteousness' — a process involving the projection of an image of ultra-conservatism, characterised as 'refulgent respectability'. 'In donning the breast-plate of righteousness, the covert deviant assumes a protective shield of superiority. His armour has a particularly shiny quality, a refulgence, which tends to blind the audience to certain of his practices. To others in his everyday world, he is not only normal but righteous — an example of good behaviour and right thinking.' 'Tearoom Trade: A Study of Homosexual Encounters in Public Places', London, Duckworth, 1970.

37 It has been disputed in law whether such an offence as attempting to make a demand can exist. The Court of Criminal Appeal stated in 'R.v. Moran' (1952) 36 Cr. App.R.10, that there could not be an attempted demand: 'there is either a demand or there is not'. P.J. Pace has examined the legalities of these arguments and compared them with the more recent case of 'R.v. Treacy' (1970) 1 All E.R. 205. which decided whether the accused had been rightly convicted of blackmail. The appellant had posted a demanding letter in the Isle of Wight to someone in Germany. The appeal was dismissed, and for a second time when taken to the House of Lords ('Treacy v. DPP' (1971) 1 All E.R. 110). A broad position has been established in law that there 'can be a completed offence under S.21 even though the menaces have not operated on the intended victim'. Demanding with menaces, 'New Law Journal'. vol. 121, 1971.

38 'The Times', 7 December 1926.

39 Phenomenologically — in terms of the victim's reaction to the blackmailer's proposition — the truth or falsity of the information is of great importance, but a 'guilty mind' is not the same thing as demonstrable responsibility.

40 E. Graham, 'Lord Darling and His Famous Trials: An Authoritative Biography Prepared (For Publication) Under the Personal Supervision of Lord Darling', London, Hutchinson, 1925. It was Chicago May who said, 'Most of the Johns pay, and pay dearly, according to their means. Few have guts enough to commit suicide.' C. Hamilton (ed.), 'Men of the Underworld: The Professional Criminal's Own Story', London, Gollancz, 1953.

41 'The Times', 16 September 1932.

42 The Committee also reported: 'The work of private detectives is of exceptional concern for us because invasion of privacy is the essence of it. If privacy is to be given greater protection it would, on the face of it, seem necessary to have special regard to persons or organisations who hold themselves out to invade privacy for reward.'

'Report of The Committee on Privacy', London, HMSO, 1972, Cmnd 5012.
43 M. Litchfield, Black marks for the carbon paper pushers, 'Focus', vol. 4, 1969.
44 Price of silence: woman welfare worker blackmailed, 'The Times', 9 February 1938.

Chapter 5 Blackmail as a Social Relationship

1 'Crime and Justice in Society', Boston, Little, Brown & Co., 1969.
2 An excellent fictional account of a blackmail transaction occurs in L. P. Hartley's, 'The Betrayal', London, Sphere Books, 1969. The ageing novelist, Richard, enjoys giving extra presents of money to his private secretary, Denys, from time to time. Denys is writing a biography of Richard and he suddenly reveals that he is in possession of prejudicial information concerning Richard's past, which will not be included in the forthcoming publication if he is given more money. After paying up, Richard reflects on the changed relationship between Denys and himself: 'it made a difference now, when the money was not being offered but demanded, and demanded with threats, when it was blackmail, to use an ugly word which the modern age, with all its sympathy for criminals, hadn't quite succeeded in making pretty. "Never, never let yourself get used to anything ugly", his mother had implored him: "don't look at the M!" There was an M in blackmail as there was in money, but he would have to get used to it'.
    A second valuable literary example can be found in Iris Murdoch, 'The Nice and The Good', Harmondsworth, Penguin, 1969.
3 'The Times', 10 December 1898.
4 The definitive theoretical treatment of status passage appears in B.G. Glaser and A.L. Strauss, 'Status Passage', London, Routledge & Kegan Paul, 1971. Glaser and Strauss characterise the form to which we are referring as 'undesirable for the passage' (i.e. the putative blackmailer), but desirable for 'the agent' (i.e. the complainant, the police, and the courts). 'When the status passage is desirable only for the agent, then recalcitrance and conflict are likely to dominate it. Whether the agent tries to persuade the passage to cooperate or forces him to go along with the passage depends upon the kind of power he has at hand and whether the situation is appropriate for its use. Usually, the agent possesses a combination of powers for gaining some measure of compliance and cooperation.'
5 Questions addressed to Montagu Noel Newton, one of the conspirators in the blackmail of 'Mr A'. C.E. Bechhofer Roberts describes Newton

in these terms: 'Confidence-trickster, blackmailer, card-sharper, forger, Newton was the real success of the trial. Dapper, neat, self-assured, wearing a different suit each day, he told his story with an air of complete frankness and no silly concessions to Mrs Grundy or any other of the invisible potentates interested in the proceedings'. 'The Mr A Case', London, Jarrolds, 1950.

6 M.B. Scott and S.M. Lyman, Accounts, 'American Sociological Review' vol. XXXIII, 1968. 'Like excuses, justifications are socially approved vocabularies that neutralise an act or its consequences when one or both are called into question. But here is the crucial difference: to justify an act is to assert its positive value in the face of a claim to the contrary. Justifications recognise a general sense in which the act in question is impermissible, but claim that the particular occasion permits or requires the very act.' By contrast excuses are 'accounts in which one admits that the act in question is bad, wrong or inappropriate but denies full responsibility'.

7 Goffman has enlarged upon the remedial functions of apologies, serving as social tools to rescue a pattern of relations damaged by some rule infraction, thus preserving overt 'public order'. E. Goffman, 'Relations in Public: Microstudies of The Public Order', London, Allen Lane the Penguin Press, 1971.

8 Sociologists studying law have often observed a strong consensual element underlying certain legal proscriptions (e.g. against murder, blackmail, etc.), and have suggested that this reflects common agreement about the socially reprehensible nature of the behaviour concerned.

9 'The Times', 7 February 1934.

10 'The Times', 20 November 1935.

11 C.H. McCaghy, Drinking and deviance disavowal: the case of child molesters, 'Social Problems', vol. 16, 1968.

12 'A recurring issue in social relations is the refusal of those who are viewed as deviant to concur in the verdict. Or, if in some sense it can be said that they do concur, they usually place a very different interpretation on the fact or allegation than do their judges.' F. Davis, Deviance disavowal: the management of strained interaction by the visibly handicapped, 'Social Problems', vol. 9, 1961.

13 S.T. Felstead, (edited by Lady Muir), 'Sir Richard Muir: A Memoir of a Public Prosecutor', London, John Lane the Bodley Head, 1927.

14 W.R. Harrison, 'Suspect Documents: Their Scientific Examination', London, Sweet & Maxwell, 1958.

15 E.S. Turner, 'The Shocking History of Advertising', Harmondsworth, Penguin, 1965.

16 'The Times', 17, 22, 29 November, 3, 16, 29, 20, 21 December 1898.

17 In quite a different context, that of organised repressive violence, Troy Duster has spelt out one of the significant pre-conditions of guilt-free acts against other fellows: the denial of full humanity to potential victims. Once the organisational aims of a society are treated as superior to individuals, acts of evil become justified in relation to these imperatives. There is a merging of individual responsibility with the organisation and its fate. We all recognise this in the familiar adage: 'I don't give the orders, I just pull the levers'. See T. Duster, Conditions for guilt free massacre, in N. Conford and L. Comstock (eds), 'Sanctions for Evil', San Francisco, Jossey Bass, 1971.

18 'The Times', 21 December 1898.

19 Kathrin Perutz, 'Beyond The Looking Glass: Life in The Beauty Culture', Harmondsworth, Penguin, 1971, writes, 'Beauty is an eleven-billion dollar industry and the largest advertiser in America. As a theme, it goes from aesthetics to statistics and takes in almost every aspet of self-presentation. It is the ground that makes up fields of anthropology, sociology, psychology, marketing, literature, art, psychoanalysis, fashion and more . . . The beauty culture provides a modern quest for youth and love, the hope of seeming what one has not become, and a chance to disappear into the fabled America of wealth and liberty.'

20 Rachel Leverson frequently crops up in criminal biographies. Two interesting sources are: H. Wyndham, 'Blotted 'Scutcheons: Some Society Causes Célèbres'. London, Hutchinson, 1926; and E. Jenkins, 'Six Criminal Women', London, Sampson Low, 1949. Wilkie Collins used her as the model for Mrs Oldershaw, confidante of the unscrupulous Lydia Gwilt in his novel, 'Armadale'. See K. Robinson, 'Wilkie Collins: A Biography', London, Bodley Head, 1951.

21 Jenkins, op. cit.

22 'The Times', 21, 28, 29 March 1899.

23 'Thorne Motor Trade Association and Another'. All E.L.R., vol. 3, 1937.

24 Ibid.

25 J. Smith and B. Hogan, 'Criminal Law', London, Butterworths, 1965.

26 Ibid.

27 'The Times', 28 November 1899.

28 'The Times', 18 December 1891.

29 'The Times', 29 April 1895.

30 'The Times', 20 May 1892.

31 Cornish rector blackmailed, churchwarden sent to penal servitude, 'The Times', 2 November 1930.

32 'The Times', 28 April 1891.

33 'The Times', 15 November 1923.

34 'The Times', 16 June 1926.

35 Quite a different matter from a mass moral crusade against, for example, the evils of drink. Cf. J.R. Gusfield, 'Symbolic Crusade: Status Politics and The American Temperance Movement', Urbana and London, University of Illinois Press, 1963.

36 'The Times', 13 June 1899.

37 'The Times', 26 May, 2 November 1925.

38 'The Times', 27 November 1897.

39 From Extracts From A Notebook, quoted by Tony Parker, 'A Man Of Good Abilities', London, Hutchinson, 1967.

40 'The High Window', Harmondsworth, Penguin, 1959.

Index

Index